SOMETHING IN A CARDBOARD BOX

Tales from the Wildlife Hospital

LES STOCKER

Author of
The Complete Hedgehog

Chatto & Windus
LONDON

Published in 1989 by
Chatto & Windus Limited
30 Bedford Square
London WC1B 3SG

A CIP catalogue record for this book is available from the
British Library.

ISBN 0 7011 3329 5 Paperback
ISBN 0 7011 3528 X Hardback

Design by Roger Lightfoot

Photoset by Rowland Phototypesetting Limited
Bury St Edmunds, Suffolk
Printed in Great Britain by
Redwood Burn Limited
Trowbridge, Wiltshire

SOMETHING IN A CARDBOARD BOX

Contents

Acknowledgements

The wild bird or animal when it is sick or injured is alone, left to suffer its private agonies until one of us happens upon it and rescues it. Its life can often be saved, the agony subsides, it can be released back to its world. It won't say thank you but I would like to thank all those wonderful people who have taken the time and trouble to help a stricken wild animal anywhere in the world. And it's not just on behalf of the animal or bird, for, without the intervention of these samaritans, my life would not have been enriched by meeting all those courageous creatures.

My wife, Sue, and son, Colin, have stood with me from the start and kept the tea flowing. Without them I would never have succeeded in getting through the long hours it takes to look after wildlife casualties.

But it has been worth it and with the backing and improvisation of our local vets, Richard Hill, Chris Troughton and my now constant co-worker, Russell Kilshaw, we have proved to a sceptical scientific Britain that wildlife can, and should, be saved.

Once again I am thankful to Catherine Cummings for typing page after page of manuscript. Ian Mackay has once more added so much to my book with his drawings which, together with the photographs of Barry Keen, Russell Kilshaw and others listed below, illustrate where words or my own photos fail me. Thanks, too, to Guy Troughton for the Wildlife Hospital Trust Appeal logos.

My dream is for Britain's own wildlife teaching hospital to stand for all time, and now, thanks to Wildlife Hospital Trust stalwarts like Philip Dunn, Roy Collins, Jenny Babb, Andy Walton, Roger Laishley, and all our volunteer team, the first bricks are being gathered on land given to my animals by an old friend, Rob Clarke of Royco Corporation.

Thank you all for helping Britain's wild animals and birds – and please keep looking around, just in case another needs your help.

PHOTO CREDITS I am grateful to the following for use of their photographs: Barry Keen, Bucks & Herts Newspapers (pages 11, 79, 111, 120, 123, 135, 149, 157, 199, 202, 215); Russell Kilshaw (pages 129, 134, 142, 177, 192); Arthur Sidey (pages 67, 115); Nigel Brock (pages 27, 98, 208 *top rt*); *Echo & Post*, Hemel Hempstead (page 55); Philip Ide (page 112); Universal Pictorial Press (page 165); U.P. Group (page 167); Michael Hollist, *Daily Mail* (page 222).

One Friday in May

As I sped through the Hertfordshire country lanes at 60 mph I was looking for a panda. No, not the wide-eyed black and white animal from China, but the typically British small police patrol car with its flashing blue light, that was, I hoped, keeping watch over one of our own black and white in need of urgent help. Somehow I had managed to cover the miles to my rendezvous in as many minutes, but then it was only six-thirty in the morning when the Hemel Hempstead police called to report the badger injured by a hit-and-run driver.

It was just as well the two police patrolmen had agreed to stay and protect my casualty, for when I pulled up at the roadside the badger still lay where it had fallen, a pathetic, vulnerable bundle, huddled one third of the way across a very busy woodland road. Even at that time in the morning there was a constant stream of commuters speeding to their offices and factories, but that bright blinking blue light was damping their excesses and saving the badger from further harm.

It appeared, from a distance, to be a small female who was apparently quite severely stunned, as she showed no reaction to my car door opening or the click of the tailgate as I took out my badger-handling equipment. I could see the rise and fall of her chest. She was still alive. She would obviously be in deep shock, apart from any physical injuries she might have received, so I had to work quickly to get her off the cold tarmac into a carrying basket covered with warming towels.

As soon as possible, get an injured animal onto oral nourishment.

She appeared oblivious to my approach but I dared not take any chances. I intended to lift her by her scruff and rump into the carrying basket, but the slightest mistake or hesitation could still result in my getting bitten badly. Even an apparently unconscious badger can turn like lightning. So, taking every precaution, I gently touched her head with my 'badger stick' which I use for holding badgers, not for hitting them. She did not react. I covered her jaws with my stick, holding them closed. With my free right hand I gradually took hold of the fur and skin at the scruff of her neck, until I felt in control of her head. Then, dropping the stick, I grasped her rump to support her weight and lifted her into my battered carrying basket. However, she made no attempt to fight me. It seemed that, like all badger casualties, she had turned to face the oncoming vehicle and had suffered severe concussion for her valour.

I loaded her quickly into the back of the car, retrieved my 'badger stick', thanked the two patient policemen and headed, this time more sedately, back to Aylesbury, a journey of about fifteen miles.

The badger would need veterinary examination and attention so,

The two resident badgers, Biddy and Granny.

as soon as I reached home and our wildlife hospital I had Sue, my wife, phone the vet at home, before he set out for his surgery. Russell Kilshaw now carries out almost all of the Wildlife Hospital Trust's veterinary work for us and it is his pioneering efforts for our badger casualties that has enabled us to save so many seemingly hopeless cases. As it is, Russell works for a very large, busy veterinary practice, so we have to co-ordinate most of our wildlife cases for consultation in his after-surgery hours. This little female badger needed immediate treatment if she was to survive, however, so we arranged to meet at the practice well before Russell's first domestic client was due.

Eight-thirty saw Russell putting on his green operating gown as we discussed the best way to examine her and treat any wounds. Meanwhile the badger was starting to recover slightly from her concussion and, at last, was showing an interest in her predicament. We would have to anaesthetise her for examination and treatment, both for her comfort and our safety. It took Russell twenty minutes to clean up her wounds and then it was back into the basket for her to

ACTION

Road casualties
Large mammals

Make yourself obvious to other traffic

Using a large stick or piece of wood, gently lever the casualty to the side of the road. A fox or badger will bite, so make no attempt to handle them.

Drop a blanket or coat over the casualty to keep it warm.

Leave somebody to watch the animal while you go to phone the police who will recommend a rescue centre.

STAY at the site until help arrives, even if the animal has fled.

wake up before being taken back to our hospital for peace and recuperation.

As I pulled into our driveway Sue was waiting with the next badger call – it was still barely nine o'clock in the morning. I had, first of all, to settle this badger into a warm pen with an overhead heater to help her over the trauma of the last few hours. It was getting somewhat cramped in our small suburban garden which, for the time being, served as a hospital and exercise area. There were three muntjac deer trying to demolish the lawn, and a fox recovering from a road traffic accident; another pen housed the badger I had rescued the day before; our two resident badgers, Biddy and Granny, owned the whole of one side of the paved area; various cages housed a mink, stoat and squirrels; and the rear was occupied by two very large swans. The new chalet, bought for us by British Telecom and to become the surgery, was still empty – that is, if you ignored the piles of bric-à-brac and jumble stored for fundraising. A large box I had made especially for badgers could be divided in two so, after settling my patient into her half, I made a hasty repair to my now precarious carrying basket, grabbed my first cup of tea of the day and set out, hot foot, for Princes Risborough, about nine miles out of town in the opposite direction to my earlier rescue.

This second badger, unlike the female, was far from comatose. A large boar, he had commandeered the back porch of a small town house, successfully blocking the doorway and denying the lady of the house access to her utility room and back garden. Snoring one moment, then groaning and growling, the badger was not letting anyone onto his new domain. He appeared to have been badly lacerated around the rump, neck and ears – injuries typical of a run-in with dogs, probably in the terrible practice of badger-baiting. Unlike most unfortunate victims, this one had obviously escaped with his life, but with his wounds becoming infected and his home destroyed he had crawled around, getting more and more fraught until, at the end of his tether, he had come across his present sanctuary away from the strange noises and smells of the town.

Over the years I have had plenty of experience in handling boar badgers but I still treat each encounter with trepidation. This animal has the power and tenacity to move objects more than twice its own weight. Its jaws, when clamped shut, can only be opened by breaking them. It has no weak points and can curl up in an instant to mangle an unwary hand, and it makes a regular habit of bulldozing through wooden fences rather than going under or over them. A virtual powerhouse on four legs and, even though this one needed treatment, I showed a very healthy respect for his capabilities. This was not the moment to approach and prod with my badger stick. This time I would use my brand new animal 'grasper'. My previous grasper had had its sprung-steel noose bitten clean in two by a very similar badger, but the manufacturer of my new one assured me that its steel cable had been tested on the largest of dogs and was equal to any badger attack.

I was about to put his claims to the test. I wished I had time to cross my fingers, but as soon as I slipped the noose over his head and pulled it tight enough to grip him I had, on the end of a frighteningly short pole, thirty-five pounds of writhing, snapping fury. I had no time to think about the steel cable: making sure my grip on the grasper

The grasper at work.

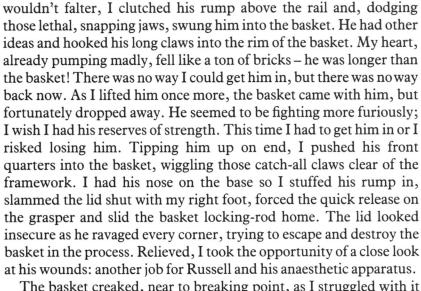

wouldn't falter, I clutched his rump above the rail and, dodging those lethal, snapping jaws, swung him into the basket. He had other ideas and hooked his long claws into the rim of the basket. My heart, already pumping madly, fell like a ton of bricks – he was longer than the basket! There was no way I could get him in, but there was no way back now. As I lifted him once more, the basket came with him, but fortunately dropped away. He seemed to be fighting more furiously; I wish I had his reserves of strength. This time I had to get him in or I risked losing him. Tipping him up on end, I pushed his front quarters into the basket, wiggling those catch-all claws clear of the framework. I had his nose on the base so I stuffed his rump in, slammed the lid shut with my right foot, forced the quick release on the grasper and slid the basket locking-rod home. The lid looked insecure as he ravaged every corner, trying to escape and destroy the basket in the process. Relieved, I took the opportunity of a close look at his wounds: another job for Russell and his anaesthetic apparatus.

The basket creaked, near to breaking point, as I struggled with it to the car. Most of the street's inhabitants had now arrived on the scene, hoping to catch a glimpse of the behemoth which had terrorised No. 9.

Never being one to waste mileage, I interrupted my drive back to Aylesbury to call in at the local goat farm to pick up the week's supply of milk for the baby muntjac we were hand-rearing. As I opened my tailgate to load the milk, there were growls from the badger and 'oohs' and 'aahs' from the farm-workers who had never been that close to a badger before.

By this time Russell was up to his eyes in cats, dogs and guinea pigs and as my latest casualty was not in a life-threatening predicament we arranged to wrestle with him during the afternoon, after the surgery's steady stream of clients had receded. In the meantime, my badger was trying his damnedest to get out of the basket so, rather than run the gauntlet of the grasper again, I gently but literally tipped him into a more substantial holding cage for the rest of the day.

The morning was now flying by. I had not even thought about my daily chores around the hospital or of the clean-up which was needed in the wake of two swans who had arrived after flying into power-

Bright Eyes

The Magazine of the Wildlife Hospitals Trust

Dinner time for hedgehogs.

lines and blacking out a small town in the process. With the help of the three muntjac they were slowly turning our small lawn into a quagmire and plastering all the paths and yard area with a mixture of mud, guano, corn and hay. Every morning the yard received a jolly good scrub and hose down, but not until I had had my four Weetabix.

Our hedgehog intensive care unit, St Tiggywinkles, was three-quarters full of equally mucky hedgehogs, all scrabbling for fresh food, water and bedding, but, fortunately, young Chris Kirk had a day off school and relished being up to his elbows changing dirty hedgehog bedding.

Our ex-dining room, which served as the office complex, was by then humming with activity as some of our team of volunteers got down to work: Catherine, sitting on the bottom stair, was completing the final edit of *Bright Eyes*, the Wildlife Hospital Trust's magazine; Lana was sorting the latest hedgehog sponsorships and demanding printing from my ever-temperamental photocopier; Sue Dunphy was in the centre of the floor unpacking the latest delivery of goods for our mail order lists and scattering polystyrene beans everywhere; while in the midst of this controlled mayhem, my wife Sue was coping with the ever-clamouring telephones and our two Cavalier spaniels, who wanted to take part and lick everybody in the process.

I finished my breakfast and outside chores and sneaked in to do my penance in administration, to a chorus of 'Can you print me some more adoption forms?', 'I need a few more lines of copy' and 'We are forty-eight rubbers short'. Even the dogs started barking, to herald the arrival of the first cardboard box of the day.

Found injured by the roadside, the box's tenant, a collared dove, had been brought to the hospital by, inevitably, a whole family, children as well. We knew what was coming: 'Have you got many animals inside? Can we have a look around?' Apart from the fact that we're very busy, our patients are all wild animals which panic at the mere approach of a human being, so we have learnt to say 'no' nicely, without, I hope, offending. Once the door was closed, I had a good excuse to flee the office and tend to our latest arrival. Safely ensconced in our small surgery unit, I could carry out a quick preliminary check of the bird's condition. The golden rule with wild birds is to handle them as little as possible to allay the initial shock, which can kill most casualties. The broken wing was obvious but I would not deal with it until tomorrow. For now I settled the little dove with the other small casualties in a warm hospital cage where it soon relaxed with the others and tucked into a bowl of best British finch mixture as though its trauma had never happened.

Then I had to find the time for a quick, late lunch of the inevitable jam sandwiches to prepare me for the furore of the office, hoping all the time for a call from Russell to extricate me from all that paperwork.

It is at busy times like this that alarm bells ring subconsciously in my head: I started the wildlife hospital because I had seen so many animals die, forgotten and alone, without anybody seeming to care. Yet my initial fears showed that our local problems were only the tip of the iceberg; there were literally millions of wild animals and birds being injured each year, and as we pushed out more and more publicity, more and more casualties started to pour in. There were heartbreaks, there were elations, but ominously as the numbers of patients rose, so did the mountains of paperwork. I could see myself fast becoming an office wallah again, away from the animals which had become one of my main 'raisons d'être'. My alarm bells remind me that others can do the paperwork just as well as I can, so now Sue and her team cope perfectly well without me most of the time and take great delight in dismissing me back to my animals.

Now the office needed me but as I half-listened in to Sue's constant telephone conversations about hedgehogs and baby birds, I picked up the word 'fox' and was nearly out of the room before Sue could give me the details. However, my relief at getting out of the office turned to horror and urgency when Sue told me a fox had been seen strangling in that most hideous of man-made devices, a snare, at the rear of Green Park, one of the most picturesque parts of the village of Aston Clinton nestling in the folds of the Chiltern Hills about five miles away. That the human race, while creating beautiful places like Green Park, can allow some of its members to scar the countryside with snares and other instruments of torture really horrifies me. When an animal is trapped by the neck in a snare, it struggles to escape and nearly strangles itself. It passes out and the snare releases, allowing the animal to recover enough to struggle some more, half strangle itself and pass out again. This horrifying 'piano wire' torment continues until the devil who set the snare comes along and rudely dispatches the animal, usually with a few blows from a blunt instrument. Unless, that is, somebody with a modicum of humanity happens upon the grisly scene and manages to release the victim.

Taking Chris with me and equipped with the grasper and, this time, a camera, I sped as fast as possible to Green Park. Once there, we were led by the Principal of the Training Centre for about half a mile along overgrown banks of the disused Wendover Canal. It was pure luck that the unfortunate fox had been spotted at all in this out-of-the-way site. It was a long wire which held him as he struggled to get away from our approach. I could see it tightening as he pulled; there was no way I could ease that pain other than by catching him and cutting away the garrotte. As we stopped to discuss our tactics, he too stopped and looked at us. For a moment the strain was off, so I quickly photographed his situation as an indictment of legitimate, so-called country sports. But was this legitimate? This snare had been fixed on top of an obviously active badger sett and, while any fiend can do what they like to foxes, there is legislation to protect badgers. Yet my experience has shown that foxes, being of a slighter frame, suffer far more than any badger would.

Now was was not the time to get on my 'soap box'. The fox needed rescuing. So I approached slowly, the now petrified fox straining at the limit of his wire noose. His ears flat and bowels loose, he tried vainly to escape from me but the snare held him tight, choking, relentless in its torture. Breaking down the undergrowth, I made a measured lunge and slipped the noose of my grasper over his head. Two nooses were now biting into his neck. He wanted to bite back but I clutched the scruff of his neck quickly, released my grasper and held him like a passive, giant kitten as Chris cut away the choking wire. I wanted to release him there and then but I had seen the internal damage a snare can do so would take him back as another casualty for Russell to check.

As I put him in the basket and covered it with a towel I tried to comfort him in his terror by telling him that he would soon be free. Naturally he did not take any notice. But then, why should foxes ever trust human beings, many of whom relentlessly persecute them on the trumped-up charge of being vermin? The fox is Britain's main predator, like the tiger in Asia and the lion in Africa, yet it is the tigers and lions which are offered protection in spite of their occasional man-eating misdemeanours. I cannot understand how people can

A fox in trouble.

hunt the fox, a sprinter, with marathon-running hounds, and still insist that it enjoys the chase. I have never known any animal show as much fear as does the fox and I wonder just how many die of heart failure from over-exertion, even if they do escape the flesh-ripping jaws of their pursuers.

I'm back on my 'soap box' again and losing my temper, just as I did then, cutting every trace of that snare from the badger sett. I cut each inch of it into tiny pieces, leaving my calling card for the coward who had set it in the first place. Meticulously, Chris and I searched all around the sett and neighbouring undergrowth to see if any other traps had been placed, and we were relieved to find none.

Before leaving we left a message for the landowner about the villainous trespassing going on around his farm and a brief note on the laws relating to the persecution of badgers. In fact, Britain's wildlife laws are a joke. Other countries laugh at us while we sit back and rest on our laurels as a 'nation of animal lovers'. We are so far behind the rest of the world that even under-developed nations are leaving us standing; if any effort is made to change things, the moves are somehow blocked by the very people who seem to enjoy making a travesty of the fox's life. Only recently, when moves were made by Britain in the European Parliament to have the evils of bullfighting exposed, Spain simply sent their TV crews to film the barbarism of foxhunting as a 'pot-calling-the-kettle-black' exercise.

Back at the hospital, I took a quick peek at the fox who was now curled up, looking quite comfortable in the carrying basket. Knowing that I would soon be going to the vet's surgery, and so as not to handle him unnecessarily, I left him in the covered basket in a quiet corner of the garden. Meanwhile Lyn, another of Sue's team of volunteers, had arrived to pick up her correspondence. An opportune moment because Lyn is an avid badger watcher, spending many cold, draughty nights huddled uncomfortably, enthralled by the comings and goings at various badger setts around the county. She was as appalled as we were at the snare on Green Park and willingly agreed to keep a close watch on the night-time activity at the sett. She also agreed to take for release some of the hedgehogs to which we had given five-star hotel accommodation throughout the winter period.

No. 1 Pemberton Close looks just like any other house . . .

The early weeks of May, when the first swifts are arriving, is the ideal time to release hedgehogs. Every winter we keep any late casualties through to the spring so that they do not have to face the perils of hibernation. Swifts are luckier: not having to hibernate they make phenomenal journeys to and from southern Africa, but when they arrive back in Britain many become grounded – not because they are injured but simply because they are designed for an aerial existence and cannot take off from ground level. We have many brought to the front door in cardboard boxes. The birds are then simply carried through the house and launched into the air out of the back door. We never tell the rescuers for fear of embarrassing them or deterring them from picking up another swift which might just need attention.

The secret of a successful swift-launch is literally to throw it as high as possible. It can then unfurl those scimitar wings, find itself a thermal and disappear into – dare I say it? – the wide blue yonder.

Hedgehog releasing is a bit more involved, needing the right garden habitat to sustain their enormous appetites. Happily, most of our team have large, suitable gardens, so, recycling some of the discarded cardboard boxes from the skip, I was able to round up

quite a few for release. Sue Dunphy would take three to her house in Tring, Catherine four to Leighton Buzzard and Lana, who has an enclosed garden, would take the three-legged convalescent not suitable for release into a fully wild environment.

I had just said goodbye to all the volunteers and their hedgehogs, and sat down, pen poised, at my desk when Russell rang to say he was ready for my next two patients. It was four-thirty.

No problem loading the fox into the car: he was still curled up, apparently comfortable in the carrying basket. But Horatio, as we had christened the enormous boar badger, was a different matter altogether, and I didn't relish the thought of another skirmish with him. It all sounds very straightforward: badger in cage to be transferred to carrying basket. That is, until your badger suddenly recognises the grasper and decides not to play ball. Running true to form, as I slid the grasper through the gap in the cage front, Horatio saw it coming and tucked his head onto his chest, offering me a large hairy back with nowhere to get a secure hold. I slid it under his head, over his back, under his rump. I even tried to push it between his chin and chest, all to no avail: he was not going to be caught out. However, I am a little bit wiser than badgers and had an ace up my sleeve. Putting the grasper in front of his head I gently touched his rump with my badger stick. He looked up for a moment to see what was going on and 'bingo!', I had the noose over his head and ears and yanked it tight. He bucked, kicked, growled and bit, but I had him fast and, clutching his rump with my free hand, I dumped him rather ignominiously into the basket once again, slamming the lid shut with my foot. So precarious was the state of the basket that, had I picked it up by the handle on the lid, I felt sure it would have split asunder, giving Horatio the freedom to run riot round the hospital. As it was, I had to carry it two-handed by the base, a daunting experience with Horatio grinning only inches from my face. It was a relief when he was in the back of the car and covered up.

I struggled through the rush hour to Russell's surgery in the town centre, fully expecting a fully grown, now very irate boar badger to come hurtling over the back seat at any minute. It seemed to take forever for me to cross every road junction and, as usual, the High

Swifts have to be launched from the hand.

ACTION

Recipe for Wildlife Hospital Trust Glop

Suitable for bats, raising some baby birds and weaning hedgehogs and other small meat-eating mammals:

- cup Pedigree Chum Puppy food
- cup Dried Insect Food (Sluis Universal or Haiths Prosecto)
- cup cold water
- ½ teaspoon multi-vitamin powder (SA37 or Millpledge Vetamin)
- ¼ teaspoon bone meal feed
- ¼ teaspoon Can-Addase Enzyme (available through vets)

Liquidise till smooth and the consistency of soft ice cream. Should be discarded after 24 hours.

Street was blocked with cars parked haphazardly, their owners collecting McDonald's takeaways. I got there at last, managed to park, then burst into the waiting room with my bulging carrying baskets. It all went quiet; the dog and cat clients had never seen a badger before, let alone one which was threatening to eat a wire basket right before their eyes. Russell saw my predicament and quickly ushered me through the 'Private. No admittance' door at the rear of the waiting room.

We were in the heavy, sauna atmosphere of the Prep Room. The steriliser steamed away, wisps of anaesthetic and disinfectant hung in the air and two large recumbent dogs with fresh operation scars lay across the gangway. I stepped over them; one coughed and spluttered and a nurse removed its endo-tracheal tube, before another success was carried off to the recovery room.

Both my patients were fully alert to all the new smells and now the fox joined Horatio in trying to eat its carrying basket. Their own warning scents overpowered those of the surgery. Some of the nurses complained and didn't look convinced when I explained that our human scent is probably far more obnoxious to the delicate noses of these wild animals.

The fox was going to be the easier to handle and might not need medical attention, so we decided to deal with him first. I prefer to handle foxes using my badger stick. A fox's neck is far more delicate than a badger's, which is why so many suffer horribly in snares, whereas badgers sometimes come off unscathed, and why I try not to resort to the grasper. My badger stick, which now shows the teeth marks of many encounters with badgers and foxes, is ideal for diverting or intercepting an animal's jaws while I get a good grip on the scruff of the neck. I had tried many types of stick but this one has proved ideal. It is the large remnant of one of the 'plonkers' used by Morris Dancers, which had broken during a particularly hectic 'stick dance' and is now banded by fluorescent tape as a precaution against leaving it, unobserved, on a night-time badger rescue.

The fox knew I was coming, he cowered in the corner of the basket as I slid my stick in under the lid. He snapped at the stick, I pushed it against the top of his mouth and held him while, with my other hand,

I felt and gripped a good handful of scruff just behind his ears. As I lifted him he relaxed like a kitten. But the fear was still there. He defecated again. Russell moved quickly and tied a loop of bandage around the jaws to act as a muzzle. I transferred my grip to under its chin – holding its lower mandibles to protect Russell as he systematically manipulated the head, neck, shoulders and forelimbs, feeling for any tissue damage, fractures or dislocations. The fox seemed unharmed by his brush with the hunter's snare and could be released as soon as possible, but, for the time being, it was back into the basket with a frantic flurry as I removed the muzzling bandage.

We had been as quick as possible, but our impatient badger had become more and more irritated by his incarceration. His teeth had mangled the wire at one end of the basket and, as I lifted him onto the working table, he managed to hook one of those formidably clawed feet into the plastic bottom. It was no match for his power: with each scrabble he tore out more and more plastic. If I didn't do something quickly, he would be out of the basket and running amok amongst nurses, sleeping dogs and expensive veterinary equipment. I dropped the basket to the floor and, not being able to think of a better way of holding him, promptly sat on it. I dared not move, but somebody would have to get me another basket pretty quickly. Then the bombshell: the vets did not have another basket! I would have to get Russell to phone the wildlife hospital to ask Sue to send a replacement along with one of our neighbours.

Fortunately Horatio was concentrating on the basket's bottom, not on mine just above him. It seemed to take ages for the relief column to arrive but then the rush hour was still crawling by. At last it came. The basket looked very frail compared to the brute I was sitting on, but, if we ever did get him subdued and treated, he would still be partially anaesthetised for the journey home.

For the moment he was livelier than ever. I could hear his teeth clashing together. The bottom of the basket was now non-existent. I had to make the next move: get him out and hold him for a moment while Russell injected a sedative into his rump. Even this task which is comparatively simple where most animals are concerned is a problem with badgers. The drug of choice for immobilising animals is called, surprisingly enough, Immobilon. Comparatively cheap and easy to administer intra-muscularly it has one important drawback: it can kill a vet within fifteen minutes. Following rigid safety precautions, before he even opened the Immobilon, Russell would always draw off a hypodermic with the required amount of antidote and quite calmly show me which one of his veins to inject if there were an accident. This is all very well if you are using a dart gun, like someone in those African safari films, or injecting a teddy bear, but after one previous bucking badger had broken the needle clean off in its rump we knew we had to find a safer alternative. Although it is far more expensive we now use a drug called ketamine hydrochloride, which will not kill humans but does have the desired effect of quietening down badgers.

That is, if you can first hold your badger. Horatio had other ideas and for the next five minutes I tried every way possible to get hold of him. Six times I nearly had the grasper over his head but every time he just managed to tuck into an impregnable ball. Then he clamped his jaws onto the steel cable and tried to pull me in with him. The bottomless basket was giving me problems. I was trying to hold that down with one foot, which made it exceedingly difficult to work the grasper through the narrow gap of the lid. I tried my old touch-the-rump trick, but he knew all about that one. It was just a question of patience and intense concentration – looking and feeling all the time for a gap in his defences. I prodded, he rolled, I was in – no, he had the grasper in his jaws again. I got it over his head but over a front leg as well: I couldn't control him like that. Russell, as always, was commenting on my success or failure: 'Fifteen–love, thirty–love, to the badger.' The nurses had fled the room; obviously they thought the badger would win. But then he made his one mistake and looked up. I had him and pulled that grasper so firmly that I began to worry that I might hurt him, though I am assured that it is nigh on impossible to harm a badger with a grasper. I grabbed his rump, heaved him out of the basket and stretched him as much as my strength would allow. He fought like a demon but at my signal, and with us both watching those jaws, Russell hit home with the injection and I dumped Horatio into the new basket, slammed the lid shut,

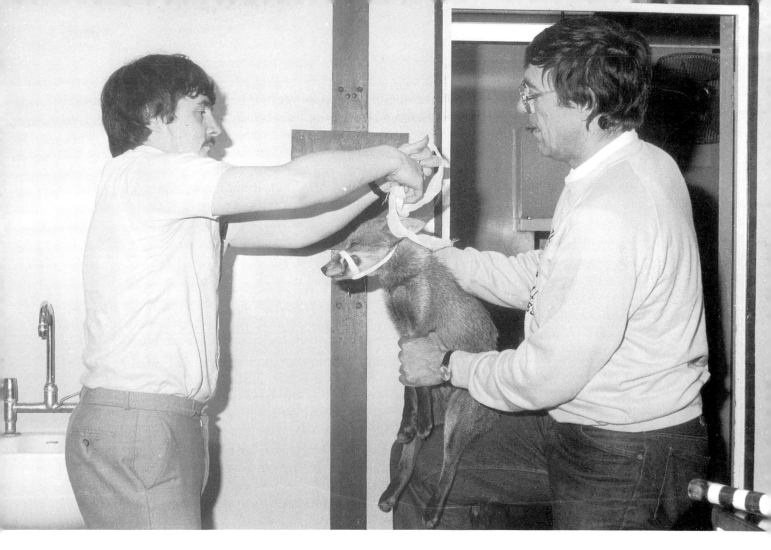

released the grasper and slid the locking-bar home. A chance now to get some breath back while the ketamine took effect.

Ten minutes later a tentative prod with the badger stick showed him to be much more approachable though still not fully co-operative.

He was still awake but far more docile. I could now, using my badger stick to hold his jaws, pull together and clasp as much scruff as his muscular neck would allow. Lifting him two-handed and under control, I could offer up his snout for Russell to muzzle. But

Russell Kilshaw quickly ties a loop of bandage around its jaws.

this is not the simple muzzling of a long pointed snout like the fox's; the badger's snout is quite short and blunt and of course more powerful. Two bandage muzzles are the order of the day, and even then the badger can have another ace up *his* sleeve: those long front claws may not be used to attack with, but they are ideal for hooking off muzzles. However, once the first bandage was in place I held the feet out of the way while the second was tied on. Then it was a question of holding his snout in the anaesthetic mask until he dropped off.

Not very elegant but effective, I thought, as I lay across him until I felt him relax. Even with aching fingers I dared not let go of that scruff until Russell had checked the reflexes.

At last Horatio was sleeping like a baby. I adjusted the anaesthetic while Russell scrubbed up and sorted his instruments. My turn to relax while Russell set to work on the wounds. It did not take long and afterwards all we had to do was wait for him to wake up – but this time stretched out in the basket: we didn't want any more wrestling with badgers. At least, not for the moment.

Back at the hospital I managed to tip Horatio gently into a large intensive care box where an overhead heater would help him recover completely from the anaesthetic. The fox could stay in his basket until we released him later that evening.

Another swift had arrived. I could hear it scrabbling to get out of his cardboard box. It seemed fully fit so, taking advantage of Sue boiling the kettle for another cup of tea, I carefully steamed its ruffled wing feathers into shape and launched it to join the other swifts screaming and diving between the houses at breakneck speed. Sue told me that John Hills-Harrop, a member of the Trust, was coming in from Chalfont St Giles with an injured hedgehog and that later Bernard Walton from the BBC Natural History Unit would be calling in to collect some hedgehogs for release around Bristol. I realised I had better have a quick meal before the evening started in earnest, and I still had my 'doctor's rounds' to do.

I'd got round nearly all the patients when John rang our raucous doorbell. The hedgehog he'd brought needed first aid to an injured leg and wouldn't co-operate. The time taken anaesthetising it gave

One of the badgers looking forward to release.

THE 3.10 London to Aylesbury thundered past — a signal to Les and Sue Stocker that the next half hour was precious. Before the next train came by, Les (right) had to free a wild badger.

Named Casey Jones, it had received skull fractures in a head on collision with a train and was nursed to health at Les and Sue's animal hospital in Aylesbury, Buckinghamshire.

This was the moment of truth would he be able to seek out his f~~~
The badger sniffed as L~~~
cage up the emb~~~

me the chance to discuss with John the film he and Mark Partridge had been making of the Trust's work. They needed some more footage of our work with hedgehogs and it did seem a pity a camera wasn't available as I cleaned up and sutured this latest casualty. We set a date for filming, then John left, taking another four of our hedgehogs for release into the salubrious gardens of Chalfont St Giles.

Horatio had recovered enough to be licking his wounds. He would be fine until I had to give him a further antibiotic injection two days later. (We really must get badgers and foxes onto antibiotic tablets concealed in their food.) The fox didn't need any antibiotics, however, and, judging by the way he had been casting voracious glances at our two resident ducks, I thought it was about time to take him out and release him.

The night was warm as Sue and I drove the fox back to his familiar territory behind Green Park. It's always a heart-searching decision when it comes to releasing a fox. What are we letting it in for? Does the hunt, thirsting after blood, make these fields unsafe? Will the fox find another snare? Is there a better place to let it go? The odds were all in favour of Green Park. He would know the territory and have it marked against other foxes; and, who knows, he may have been supporting a vixen and a bevy of wonderful cubs. He obviously knew what he wanted and, after that moment's hesitation a fox always has before leaving the open basket, he was gone, floating along the path illuminated by the car's full beam. He stopped and looked over his shoulder. I'm sure not a 'thank you', probably just checking to make sure we were not following into his secret world. Then up and over a bank, and he was gone into the dark. Good luck ol' fella.

Bernard arrived at eleven thirty. The BBC wanted to film the hedgehogs on their release. Would I advise during the filming? Certainly I would: another date for our rapidly filling calendar, but also another two hedgehogs released.

At last, a chance for a final cup of tea and then to bed, trying hard to remember how the day had started all those hours ago. The trouble is, we hadn't been in bed for long before the phone rang again. It was two o'clock – surely not another badger call? I groped down the stairs to answer it; a broad scouse accent had picked up an injured pigeon on his way home. A Liverpool pigeon is just as important as a badger but, thankfully, I could tell the samaritan how to give it first aid and look after it, over the telephone. At last I crawled back to bed, another typical day's work over – that is, if the phone did not ring again.

★

That whole weekend turned out to be extremely hectic and, by Sunday night, we had nine badgers squeezed into our tiny hospital complex. It was blatantly obvious that we really had to move on to a larger site as soon as we could. Who would ever have thought, ten years before, when we first started the hospital, that there were so many wildlife casualties which were being ignored or being put, unnecessarily, out of their so-called misery? I can still remember vividly that first patient and its lonely single aviary at the back of the garden which was to have been such a picture book garden . . .

After that moment's hesitation – he was gone.

I've Started So I'll Finish

When we first moved to Aylesbury in 1970, Sue and I had little free time to spend with each other, let alone look after injured birds and animals. But in 1978 things were to change. To start with, we decided to buy our own house. With the way house prices were rising we *had* to, it seemed, or forever miss out on owning our own home. Added to which, I then had the responsibility of Purdie, a rescued kestrel, and it was no life for her to be taken each day into the warehouse where we ran our small electrical engineering business, to sit patiently on a block until I took her home each evening, and then only to a perch. Occasionally, I was able to get away at lunchtime to the open fields and let her fly for a while. The funny thing was that I was just as loath as she was to leave that freedom and go back to work.

We took the plunge and bought a patch of mud and concrete which we were assured was going to be a house. Eventually we managed to move in, on Sue's birthday, but even then I had to leave her to unpack while I dragged my way back to the warehouse. The garden was like all gardens in new houses: the builders had removed all the top soil and left behind a quagmire of inert clay, hundreds of bricks and a particular strip of rubber which disappeared into the ground and took me two years to eradicate. I had been a very keen gardener while we were living on the outskirts of London and I envisaged

creating a similar landscape at Aylesbury, with a garden pool (an essential); rockeries of bright alpine flowers and ranks of roses for Sue to pick. But for the time it could not be, as I just did not have the time to indulge myself. Instead, a phone call to a contractor brought us instant lawns with a few rose bushes dotted along the small drive. At least, from the front window we still had a vista of neglected fields and copses where the occasional funny-coloured rabbit gambolled and a skylark sang his soaring song.

I built Purdie an aviary and set it at the bottom of the new lawn, where we could see her from the back windows. She seemed eventually to relish her new-found freedom, flying from perch to perch and going in and out of her box 'chucking' her approval to me. The birds flying over always caught her eye but she was panicked into screaming every time the motorised glider, from nearby RAF Halton, passed high in the sky. To this day she has not got used to it and still screams out, which sends our small Cavalier spaniel, Poppy, into rapturous barking because the other reason Purdie screams is when a cat is prowling by. However, she must have been comfortable and relaxed, for she soon became broody and laid four eggs. She sat and 'chucked' over them for a few days but seemed to realise they were infertile, threw them out and found new amusements by 'footing' sticks and hiding her food in various corners of her new home. She even managed to catch one or two squawking sparrows which I had to rescue in the nick of time.

Our electrical engineering business was getting busier and busier, demanding more and more of my time. Every day of the week, including Sundays, I would be away before nine and back after eight. It became harder and harder to leave my chats with Purdie every morning and, oh, how I longed to have time for breakfast.

I had been told on many occasions that the role of a managing director was to delegate. I had two very suitable members of my staff and started to ease them into taking more of my burden. It seemed to work well, I even had provisions drawn up to include them as directors of the company. Sue and I even took the opportunity to take a holiday. But things did not work out.

A business that had once been our pride and joy seemed to have

Purdie, the kestrel, would sit patiently on a block.

lost its attraction. Every day was a drudge, every cheque seemed to be for somebody else.

I just knew that I had to get out. I didn't know how or to what, but the thought of going back, every morning, to the warehouse began to drag me down to the depths of despair. The relief was that a businessman came along to buy the concern very shortly after we put it on the market. Even that had its traumas and doubts, but finally the documents were signed, I banked the cheque and contemplated my long-awaited breakfast on the patio with Purdie.

We had some money in the bank; a nice house, though the garden was dull; I had a Range Rover sitting in the drive and Sue had her little red Spitfire and a houseful of Strongbow furniture which she had always wanted. Everything seemed poised for a launch into a new life. But for some unknown reason, perhaps it was the trials of the previous year, I became ill. For week after week after week I lay on the bed. I didn't want to go anywhere, see anyone, do anything; not even read or watch the television. I didn't even think of anything; it was as though I was an empty container, drained of any use.

Sue and Colin, my son, were marvellous. They seemed to know what was going on. It is only through their support and encouragement that I began to venture out of the bedroom occasionally, look out at Purdie, whom Colin had been feeding, and watch the occasional programme on television. It was ages before I would see anybody and months before I spoke to anyone other than Sue or Colin.

I am sure now that it was only the strong bond between the three of us which pulled us up, out of that black hole. Out little world with Poppy, the dog, and Purdie was all that we wanted. All the trappings of fancy cars, fancy clothes and fancy friends seemed pointless and petty. I know that Donne said, 'No man is an island', but at that time that did seem an irresistible attraction for us as a family.

Colin was very young and had not embarked on his secondary education. We had nothing to keep us in Aylesbury. We wanted to be with the honesty of animals and birds. We did not mind where, just as long as we were together, and healthy in mind and body.

I didn't have the strength to envisage being self-sufficient again;

Colin with a young patient.

the answer appeared to be employment which required us to work with animals but without all the headaches which go with autonomy and responsibility. I had only ever had one job (before I set up my own business) and that was when I left school to work in an accountancy practice. With that and my business, where I learnt all the intricacies of domestic appliances, there was nothing substantial to put on a c.v. for an animal welfare job.

What do you always think of when you imagine a job with unlimited security, little accountability and very good wages? The Civil Service, of course. There were all these people making a wonderful living in the Nature Conservancy Council, the Forestry Commission and the Countryside Commission. How could I join them, was the question. Apparently the whole of the home Civil Service is managed on a grade system, with qualifications common to all departments. I had the necessary pieces of paper in the outside world but would have to sit an entrance examination to convert them to Civil Service jargon with a corresponding status. I had not faced an examination for fifteen years but, with Sue pacing up and down the streets of Reading outside the examination centre, I presented myself for the ordeal. I was never nervous of taking exams but, imagine my shock when I walked into a hall full of examination desks to find that I was the only candidate.

It was just like the GCE examinations I remembered: 'You may start' and at the end of the allotted time, 'Pens down'. As I was the only one writing, the adjudicator must have thought me ambidextrous, but afterwards she shared her coffee and sandwiches with me.

The papers had been on sorting logic problems, a subject on which I thrived. I passed and then had to present myself to a board of selection at a prestigious office building just off Trafalgar Square. I was then beginning to regain my confidence after all those months of indecision and told the board exactly what I wanted: to work with animals and, of course, to be successful in the Civil Service, and to change the way British wildlife was looked at. Even then, once on the subject of my animals and birds, I had so many plans and ideas that they must have thought me suitable, for I was accepted into the Civil Service, Executive Officer grade. Now for all those wonderful positions in the Nature Conservancy Council, or the Forestry Commission.

But this was not to be: the only vacancies at that grade in the whole of the Civil Service were for VAT inspectors to work out of Southend. I could not face working in an office again, with nothing other than columns of figures to tax my energies – and my experiences with Value Added Tax had been far from friendly. I replied that I was not interested in that type of position; would they let me know when something cropped up in my chosen department? The response baffled me then and still baffles me now. Apparently I would have to sit the entrance examination again, present myself once more to the Board and, if successful, would be offered a position which could once again be as a VAT inspector in Southend or anything that came up. The Civil Service did not keep waiting lists of potential applicants and would give no notification to outsiders when a position became vacant. 'Red tape', 'bureaucracy', the platitudes started to

come to mind. In spite of the security, low accountability and good wages, I did not think I could take the woolly world the Civil Service was offering and definitely did not have the fortitude or patience to keep taking that examination.

I was back to square one.

The next plan of attack was to search for advertisements in wildlife and animal papers and to write to likely organisations. However, most seemed to be working with various zoological collections or involved in 'roughing it' on obscure off-shore islands. Then a ray of hope shone out of an animal magazine: 'Couple needed to run Sussex animal sanctuary'. It could not have been better, especially when we found that it also took in the occasional wildlife casualty.

It was a long time until the interview, but when we drove up to the quaint old farmhouse set deep in Sussex woods, we knew it was worth the wait. Although in my best navy blue three-piece suit, I took the opportunity before going in to have a poke around the sanctuary. It did not appear terribly busy: only a few dogs and horses. I could have done wonderful things for animals with the facilities there.

The interview chaired by Lady Dowding – whose late husband Air Chief Marshal Dowding looked after injured blackbirds as well as master-minding victory in the Battle of Britain – and attended by other lady trustees of the sanctuary went extremely well. I went into all my plans and ideas for animals, agreed with delight at having to adopt a stray wolfhound and did not mind sharing the house with the present elderly warden, although I did not know how he would get on with Sue's David Bowie records. I was full of hope as we drove away, but a few days later came the bombshell: I was considered ideal personally for the position but I was 'too tidy and gentlemanly ever to be able to work with animals'. My accountancy training had become a distinct hindrance. Probably the fellow in the Wellington boots and duffle coat got the job.

We were getting nowhere at all. More letters, more phone calls, but nobody was doing what I wanted to do. Then we heard of a wild bird hospital in the north of England which needed somebody to help run it. Putting Purdie in the care of Sue's mum and dad, I set off with

Sue and Colin to spend two days looking at this immense possibility.

Just like our house in Aylesbury, the bird hospital in Bury was typically suburban but the façade belied the hectic crusading work going on inside. We were taken in by Mrs Irena Zalasiewicz, a wonderful lady who had survived the rigours of northern Russia to devote her life to the care of injured birds in England. Every room in the house was crammed with bird hospital, from shelf after shelf of Christmas cards in the hall, to the giant, stray macaw that had taken over the dining room. The small garden was interwoven with aviaries, housing all those British birds which were then becoming so important to me. There were rooks, crows, blackbirds, starlings and a short-eared owl with that defiant stare, so typical of the species. The garage, converted to a food preparation unit, was the territory of a very tame, blind tawny owl, probably the only bird which it is humane to keep when it has lost its sight. Tawny owls do much of their hunting by sound; their ears are set obliquely, enabling them to pinpoint the slightest rustle. Even when feeding, they close their eyes and feel their food, firstly with their talons then with the bristles around their beaks. Ollie was quite at home, walking up and down the windowsill, investigating and swallowing every morsel that was put before him.

I would have been in my element there, but Irena had another ace up her sleeve. About two miles away was an acre of prime northern woodland, complete with its own cotton-mill stream, which was to be an extension to the hospital. Already a few makeshift aviaries had been erected and a Portakabin served as kitchen and close-care facilities. We were to sleep in the Portakabin overnight, sharing it with just a few birds, including the talking magpie which lived in the toilet and passed comments to shock anyone foolish enough to use that inner sanctum.

The following morning was bright and hopeful: juvenile robins flew into the doorway for their breakfast, kingfishers excavated the banks of the stream opposite and a peculiar loud rustling from the reeds turned out to be giant dragonflies waking in the morning sun. It was a perfect day, capped with a wonderful picnic near a gigantic unspoilt man-made lake. I was falling for this in a big way, but there

Tawny owl chicks – Stan and Ollie – left destitute when their nest tree was felled.

had to be a drawback – and there was. The epitome of all I could want in life did not come with an income.

Impetuous as I was when it came to wild animals and birds, I knew that there was no way the three of us could live on air alone. Another disappointment. It was becoming more and more obvious that the only way to my chosen involvement with birds and animals would be through my own devices.

On the long drive back we had many hours in which to talk about the reversion to autonomy. We had rather relished the idea of employment with security and pension rights and all those things, but it could not be. We would have to go it alone.

I had been dabbling in freelance writing for magazines. We could sell our house and buy somewhere cheaper by the coast. We did not need two cars and, anyway, the Range Rover cost a fortune to run. There was still a fair amount of capital left over from the sale of the business and, if I really pushed out my articles, we should just about be able to make ends meet.

The house went straight on the market, the Range Rover sold easily, and we were raring to go. For month after month the 'For Sale' sign beckoned to potential buyers, but the British economy was dead. Nobody was buying houses and eventually it became an infernal nuisance to have to open the house at weekends to 'buyers', knowing that most of them were only looking for new decorating ideas, anyway. However, we persevered, re-erecting the sign after the autumn gales, the winter blizzards and the March winds had, in turn, blown it down.

We looked at houses in Devon, Cornwall, Wales, Kent, Dorset and, of course, Sussex. We looked at brochures on ancient monuments, stately homes, disused lighthouses and derelict railway stations until we unanimously set our hearts on a large house just twenty yards from the sea near Hastings, a town full of childhood memories for me of visits there with my Uncle George in his provision lorry. But still our house would not sell and, in the end, we had to pull out of our intended purchase, leaving us with a large solicitor's bill but nothing to show for it – the first large bite at our capital.

We would give it another year before trying again. Perhaps the

economy would improve, perhaps the house market would flourish again, perhaps pigs might fly. Article after article was churned out of my study. Many were to do with gardening, which gave me an excuse to get to grips with ours. I wanted a pond, surrounded by a rockery built from slabs of Portland stone which I slowly accumulated on regular visits to the two caravans we owned and let out in Swanage. I soon learnt the pitfalls of keeping a pet rabbit, as he ate the herbaceous border, ring-barked a fine eucalyptus tree and generally made any young plant's life precarious. Sadly, he had to go into a pen. Purdie was still calling to me from her aviary and a few casualties had appeared, including Hoppy our first wood pigeon, who had been run over by three different cars before he was rescued. With no expert knowledge, I splinted his broken leg and it mended, although from then on he always had a limp, hence his nickname.

A broken leg in a bird is fairly easy to diagnose and I was reasonably satisfied with my first aid, but I wanted to learn so much more. We scoured all the book lists and visited every secondhand book shop from Charing Cross Road to Bournemouth, searching for the written word on the subject of injured birds. There were a few stories of experiences with one or two species, but nothing technical. Nevertheless, I found those books so easy to read. They were all I wanted to read. Time and time again I relived with the authors their ups and those terrible downs. I became obsessed with the plight of those hapless birds and knew that I had to do something to help, but how? Since those terrible months, after the sale of our business, I still wanted to stay behind closed doors in my castle, where nobody could harm us. But isolation would do nothing to stem the suffering of injured birds.

Then fate seemed to take a hand. Some birds in Aylesbury needed help and nobody was lifting a finger. Officialdom had arranged for the town centre's pigeon population to be slaughtered because they were, supposedly, becoming a nuisance. It's funny how some people need little persuasion to revert to the gun as a 'cure all'. There weren't, in fact, very many pigeons, but why kill them anyway? After all, by building the monstrosity that is our town centre, the developers had created cliffs and ledges which were ideal pigeon

STRICTLY FOR THE BIRDS

A LOCAL bird lover has come forward with a plan to save Aylesbury's fated pigeons from almost certain death.

Because of their growing numbers the pigeons are being trapped and killed by the Aylesbury Vale Council officials who say that the birds cause considerable mess on local buildings, pavements and shop windows.

On reading of the pigeons' plight in the Advertiser, Mr Les Stocker has come up with a survival plan for the birds.

Mr Stocker, who runs a one-man Bird Rescue Society has written to the council offering his ser-
____ ____s that if

"I hate to hear of any animal or bird bein destroyed — ever the council say it humanely—so I o services", said who li

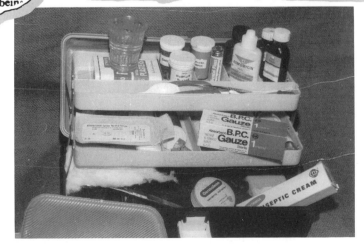

The Stockers' first wildlife hospital contained in one plastic box.

quarters. I could not let the massacre take place and came out of my reclusion, offering an alternative suggestion which involved catching the birds and moving them elsewhere. The local papers found out about my stand and soon I was festooned over every local news-stand. I was out in the open, but I *had* saved those birds. So why not stay in Aylesbury, I thought, and start to do something positive for a change, instead of merely reading books about it?

We tried various names for ourselves: 'Bird Rescue' and 'Friends of Fur and Feather', and wrote to all the local vets and RSPCA Inspectors, telling them how we were willing to care for any wild bird casualties they might encounter. I think they were all relieved at having somewhere that would take on the responsibility of wild casualties.

That was the turning point.

I got to know all the vets at Tuckett, Gray and Partners – first Richard Hill, then Chris Troughton and very soon afterwards Russell Kilshaw who now does all our veterinary work. We also struck up a lasting friendship with Charlie Norris, our local RSPCA Inspector, who over the years was to prove such an ally and mentor until his recent retirement to his home town of Ashford in Kent.

At first, not many casualties were brought in. I think that most people were still unaware that anybody really cared and many bird protection societies were still saying, 'The only way to deal with an injured bird is to bang it over the head with a heavy object.' It was going to take us years to break down that indoctrination, but eventually even these societies began passing casualty calls on to us.

I had plenty of time to concentrate on my writing and could spend many days in wild corners of the countryside, learning about its lore and beliefs, seeing for myself how the animals and birds thrived or perished and, most alarming of all, how some country people treated them. I could never understand, and still cannot, how the farmer can persecute the fox. Here is an animal which helps control the rodents which can blight a harvest; the days of free-range farm chickens are long since gone, yet still I regularly came across the hunt.

Then, of course, there are the beagle hounds and beagling, another country pursuit which should have been civilised along with witch-burning and bear-baiting after the Middle Ages. I did not even know at first what they were beagling for, and couldn't believe my ears when I found out that it was hares. The hares I had seen in the field were marvellous, proud, powerful animals, never in large groups. I fail to see how they could be regarded as vermin – for one thing, they are becoming extremely scarce. So why hunt them, and with dogs? I had to see for myself what went on.

In fact, when we turned up on 'meet day' and saw the scruffy, ramshackle mob in their green jackets, velvet riding caps, silk cravats, nearly white jodhpurs and muddy training shoes or dirty white plimsolls, we wondered if beagling wasn't, after all, some sort of obsolete music hall farce. I suppose that, if it were not for the fact that they often kill hares and leverets and, like other hunts, do considerable damage to the countryside, they could be left alone to make fools of themselves.

Before the real 'work out' began it seemed customary to sup a few pints of the local ale. There being no horses, I doubt if it was called a 'stirrup cup', but it probably had the same effect of strengthening the sinews for the horrific journey ahead.

Promptly at thirteen minutes to one, they all set off for the killing fields. I felt overdressed with my wellies on, whereas all the hunt followers had by now put on the latest in lightweight green beagling galoshes and I soon found out why. This was obviously some form of keep-fit weight-training: after the first field we were all carrying great dumb-bells of mud on our feet, which we had to swing forward even to move.

The hounds milled around sniffing the ground. Then one barked – sorry, gave voice – and they were gone. That was the last most of the followers saw of the hounds, many of which ran about haphazardly, in all directions, with no idea of which scent to pursue.

I followed the pack for a while. Well, for about five minutes, until they had disappeared into the landscape behind their invisible quarry. Alone and out of sight of the others I was suddenly confronted by the streaking hare, obviously panic-stricken by the pack behind her. Needless to say I cheered her pluck (hares are always 'she' to beagle hunters, perhaps it enhances their dominant male ego)

and stood prepared to challenge her persecutors, who were fortunately three or four fields behind her. As it turned out, the hare did not need my intervention as she was way ahead and once she had crossed the nearby road was lost in the safety of village gardens.

★

It was a relief to get back to the sanity of Aylesbury and especially to all the other people I was getting to know there: people who loved animals and birds; people who put themselves out to help; wonderful, kind people like Herb and Doris Reeves, whose life revolves around three cats and two pigeons, one of which would have been put down but for their intervention.

I have always been very fortunate that I have never had to put a bird down, not that I could. Vets and RSPCA Inspectors are trained in the *coup de grace* and the only bird I ever took in that needed euthanasia, a tawny owl with massive and malignant tumours, was humanely destroyed for me by one of the vets. As I took in more and more birds, I began to realise that unlike mammals, they seem to have an inbuilt ability to die if they want to.

Sometimes, for no apparent reason, a bird will just stop breathing, even if it has very minor injuries or none whatsoever. Herons are notorious for such self-euthanasia, but the first one I ever took in had no such intentions.

As Charlie Norris brought it through the front door, it was folded up in a basket with those cold yellow eyes looking out at me, daring me to go towards it. It looked quite small until I lifted it out. As I held its neck to keep that lethal beak at arm's length, the rest of the animal unfurled behind it: two enormous flapping wings which filled the kitchen and two gangly legs which pedalled in the air, clasping anything in their way in two enormous claws. It was like fighting Rod Hull's Emu on some children's TV programme. I hung on to the beak but, once I had grabbed one wing as well, I had no hands left to grab the other and those claws were now striking at me. He would have made a good octopus. Round the kitchen we wrestled, the cups went flying off the draining board and the heron deposited cupfuls of guano down my jeans. This was getting ridiculous. Why not tuck the wing in, under the arm that's holding the beak? Good. Grab the other

---

ACTION

Injured wild birds

Place the casualty in a warm, dark container on an old towl (*not* hay or straw). Do not offer any liquid.

After 2 hours check the casualty, its condition and the extent of its injuries.

If it is still unconscious or if there are any obvious fractures or dislocations, it should be referred to a sympathetic vet or reputable bird rescue centre.

If the bird seems fully recovered, let it fly around an enclosed room and then release it where it was found.

At all times keep the bird warm and quiet and do not offer any liquid.

wing, fold it and tuck that under. Fold one leg at a time up to the beak and hold. Eventually I had a complete heron tucked under my arm, held by one hand. Now to find a cage for him. Not easy, but he could be folded into a cat-carrying box which would keep him under wraps, at least for a while.

Somehow, Henry the heron, as he became known, had fallen into the canal, and had later been rescued by Charlie. He did not take kindly to captivity and even after I had dried him and put him into an outside aviary he panicked every time I approached, flapped his wings, tripped over his own legs and fell flat on his beak. Those legs seemed so frail that I was worried he would hurt himself. But no, as soon as I had hidden around a corner he would sort himself out, regain his dignity and stand, hunched, miserable, waiting for my next approach. The sooner I released him, I decided, the better.

I know of a heronry near Tring, overlooking three reservoirs, a canal and numerous small brooks, which would would be an ideal release site. I wrested him into a basket once more and then, taking Charlie with me, travelled to the proposed release site. Now, herons when in flight are marvellous, enormous and graceful, so I asked Charlie to let Henry go at chest height in order that I could get a photograph as he took off. I was ready, Charlie was poised and posed, and on the count of three Henry was free. But he did not take off. Instead, he calmly dropped to the ground and walked off into the distance, only to launch himself when he was out of sight behind some reeds. The only photographs I have of that elated moment of release are of Charlie about to launch Henry; Henry's back as he strode away and a little dot in the sky as he flew to join his peers. A successful release but a hopeless photographic experiment.

The site where we released Henry was one of those very rare places where nobody seemed to go – perhaps it was the 'Private. Keep Out' sign which proved effective. Sue and I made it one of our favourite haunts where I could glean material for articles while Sue could sit and sketch the plant formations which were an integral part of her abstract paintings. It was an eerie empty place, honeycombed with unusual small rivulets and lagoons and clumps of alder, where the mallards, moorhens and buntings played and rested. Half-buried

Charlie Norris with the heron poised for release.

under one tree was an old cart with wooden wheels which looked as though it had lain there for centuries. Old dead trees smothered in ivy housed wrens and funny spiders, while under the heronry heaps of discarded pellets revealed all the fish bones eaten by the youngsters trumpeting far above us. Nobody else ever went there.

One day, a friendly Water Board official spotted our car and only then did we find out why nobody ever visited the area. Apparently the whole acreage was one giant gravel-bed used by the water authorities to filter water into the nearby reservoirs. He told us about the overgrown area which was my favourite haunt, warning us: 'Nobody who ever goes in there will come out alive.' Needless to say I kept quiet about my little expeditions but Sue too was in danger as the little streams, where she dangled her feet while sketching, belied the six feet of oozing mud under their few inches of water. At that moment the rickety log bridges we had been using seemed even more precarious.

We still go back there occasionally, but only ever to release birds and small mammals for which the site is perfect. We went there the following winter, just to watch the small waders grubbing around the edges of the frozen lagoons, but we kept very strictly to the one main path.

Happily, most birds like those ones manage to cope with winter unless it is very severe. Many winter casualties are the result of extraordinary accidents or just plain 'bird brain' stupidity – like the swan that mistook the A40 London to Oxford road for a major waterway and crash-landed slap, bang, amongst the startled commuter traffic.

She slushed contentedly around the forecourt of a nearby garage which called us in to rescue . . . them, not the swan! I had never handled a swan before, I remembered all those tales of how one flap from its wings could break an arm, but it was obviously in trouble and needed my help, so off we went, armed with a large cat box.

That was my first mistake.

As I got out of the car, the garage attendants had a good laugh: 'You'll never get the swan in that box.' And how right they were. Isabella, as we named her, was nearly as tall as Sue as she stretched

For four days she stayed with us.

herself, hissing and puffing at our approach. But I was determined not to get another laugh: I was going to show the onlookers that I was used to handling even the most aggressive swan. Isabella had timed her bravado but it had failed to produce results, so she turned to run. As though I had always done it that way, I grabbed her neck, tucked her wings in and stuffed her under my arm. My antics with the heron had certainly taught me something. Too late I wondered, 'Do swans bite?' Apparently not. Isabella just squeaked and gurgled, no more hissing. Nonchalantly tossing the ridiculous box into the back seat, as laid-back as you like, I wrapped her three or four times in some old blankets, put her in the back of the car and drove off, to the cheers of the forecourt staff who could get on with selling petrol.

Back at Aylesbury, Isabella was terribly mucky when I unwrapped her in the garage. A bowl of water and a dish of soggy bread rolls were soon sat upon and scattered in every direction. The walls were smattered with the muck, Sue's washing machine and freezer had an interesting new decoration of mud, bread, water and black stuff from the petrol station forecourt. With the arrival of another bowl of water, she started to preen off the grime of her adventure.

For four days she stayed with us, defying anyone to pass her. Sue would not go near the washing machine or freezer so, for days, we lived on tinned food and potatoes. And Poppy, our Cavalier spaniel, was so terrified of the constant, hissing onslaught that she took to soiling the door mat rather than venture out into the garden.

Fortunately, after those four hectic days we were able to take Isabella out and release her on a genuine stretch of water where she had only the local ducks to harass and they soon bowed to her regal battering.

This exciting episode apart, a few other casualties were brought in. We were managing to survive on the meagre income from my articles and our now dwindling capital. Perhaps, after all, we could survive the new lifestyle . . . Then a bombshell hit us from the Inland Revenue. Isn't it funny how OHMS letters always arrive on a Saturday morning? I think they save all their posting until Friday afternoon, knowing that over the weekend they can't be contacted and you will suffer an anxiety attack. Apparently, although I had relied on professional advice at the time, the capital we received from the sale of the business was subject to far more Capital Gains Tax than had been estimated. With this fresh chunk taken out of our reserves, we could not possibly manage, and none of the entreaties I made the following week made any difference.

It seemed that all the effort we had put into building a new life had been pointless. But it hadn't: there were birds alive which would not otherwise have been and there were going to be more which needed our help. We had to find a solution, but at that period this seemed an absolute impossibility – I would have to start scouring the job columns again. And this time I would have to accept the incarceration of an office.

A Sign-On of the Times

Our short-lived love affair with the countryside seemed to be coming to an end. True, I could try to write more articles, but there were only a few magazines which published natural history material and my writing was considered somewhat 'alternative' – a constant campaigning for the underdogs of the undergrowth. But I was lucky. Each piece I produced, except those opposing blood sports, was published, and I was encouraged that prestigious journals like *Amateur Gardening* printed my crusades to protect the unloved: slugs, moles and wasps at last had a champion. I felt that my articles had a purpose and were saving wildlife, but unfortunately they could not produce enough income to support us, the birds, the animals and the overdraft. One thing set me thinking: since the euphoria of seeing my first article in print, I'd observed that my pieces were illustrated with photographs, often by the world's top natural history photographers, such as Eric Hosking, whose work I had admired for years. If I could supply photographs with my submissions, then not only would I stand more chance of having complete packages accepted, but I would also attract extra payment for the pictures.

Until then I had always been a snap-happy family-groups-on-the-beach photographer, but I decided I would have to learn to do better. Many of my subjects, however, were beyond the scope of my £50

Praktica. But, for the first of many times since then, fate took a hand and supplied the answer from a very unexpected quarter.

Each week Sue and I would take advantage of the free advertisements selling things for 'under a tenner' in the *Bucks Herald*, our local paper. Every Friday people would appear to swell our coffers very slightly by buying goods and chattels which we felt we could afford to do without. Sev – I never did learn his surname – drove a hard bargain for some surplus tools. Being exiled from Poland to Britain into the wartime RAF, Sev had learnt to face up to life and wasn't about to purchase lightly. He took all the equipment to pieces and checked it. 'Eet is worn,' he announced in his Polish accent. 'I will give you seven pounds, no more.' We knew that he meant it. Then he spotted my camera lying on the kitchen worktop. 'You take photographs. May I see them?' 'These are not goot.' When I muttered my excuses for the lack of quality, he retorted, 'Come round to my home next Thursday afternoon. I weel show you the photographs.' This was more of an order than a request.

Climbing over piles of old *Amateur Photographer* magazines and cardboard boxes (Sev was a great hoarder), I presented myself as required and soon realised that he knew more about photography than I could possibly ever know and that he was more than willing to have a go at teaching me the correct way to photograph my subjects.

I went back to school, not with a blackboard and easel but in Sev's living room where, every Thursday afternoon for month after month, he would batter me full of all the techniques, from the simplicity of the first pin-hole camera to the intricacies and complicated calculations involved in lighting minute subjects like insects and other small animals. He could tell, just by looking at a negative, how good or bad it was.

Photography can be a very expensive pastime, but Sev did not let that stand in his way, or mine. He was a superb engineer and innovator and had made most of his equipment out of scrap materials and cocoa tins. My Praktica camera was very worn and had no thread mount, which made it quite unsuitable for what we were demanding of it. Sev found some bits of wood, a few bolts and came up with a small cradle which was ideal for use on the macrophotography

transporter I had made from an old car jack, the rubber bung off a freezer compressor and various washers from the bottom of my tool box. I seemed to be catching his habits. Sev gave me my first enlarger, which he had made out of brass aeroplane parts. It sat handsomely in my improvised darkroom among the cocoa tin safe-lights, ice cream tub light-boxes, a timer I had borrowed from my father and various animal food dishes for the chemicals. It was, in reality, my study with the daylight kept at bay by an old wartime blackout curtain. This darkroom became my Everest and in spite of the mountains of discarded failures and the idiosyncrasies of the string which worked the enlarger, I started to get acceptable prints. And, what's more, they were being published. We were managing to keep in touch with the overdraft.

During the summer months our two caravans at Swanage brought in some more pennies but travelling to and from Dorset in Sue's Spitfire was becoming a joke. I could see out of it to drive only by looking over the top of the windscreen and Colin was growing so fast that we almost had to use a shoehorn to squeeze him onto the rear parcel shelf which purported to be a back seat. The car had to go, but at that moment my mother came up with a rescue plan. Having just retired she generously used a great part of her gratuity to buy something for each of her three children. Consequently, the Spitfire went and we acquired the light-blue Escort Estate which became a faithful workhorse and landmark of the early years of our wildlife rescue work.

We were comfortably mobile again but more and more birds seemed to be arriving and the overdraft was, once more, beginning to creep up. What else could we sell? I mentioned earlier that Sev was a hoarder, but that was calling the kettle black. Over the years I had collected all manner of things which were now going to stand us in good stead, starting with a large selection of silver coins, dated before 1946, which I had gleaned from my change in our early days of marriage. At the time I had collected them for their intrinsic value, but now dealers were offering to buy them at twenty times their face value. Being one of life's collectors, I was going to find it hard to part with them, but it had to be and, when we returned from the dealer with £900 to pay off the overdraft, the wrench seemed easier to bear.

My collection of old books about Aylesbury was next. Well, what did it matter? We were going to move anyway. Then it was my collection of domestic bygones, including a hand-cranked Baby Daisy vacuum cleaner and the world's first hand-operated automatic washing machine, which went to furnish a seaside castle in north Devon. I did retain, for old time's sake, one of the selections of washing 'dollies' which housewives once used to stir their washing in big stone coppers that billowed steam and suds every Monday morning. I had collected all those during my years working in domestic appliances, a period which paid off in another way, in that I was commissioned to write and illustrate a year's series of articles for the very popular *Do-it-Yourself* magazine.

Every facet of Sev's teaching was put to the test as I photographed, step by step, the repair of washing machines, fridges, freezers, vacuum cleaners and all the labour-saving devices of the kitchen. It was a long way from the natural history I wanted to write about but it taught me the patience and the discipline which are so important when writing at home. It was a struggle to meet each month's deadline but Sue was a genius at pacifying editors whenever I was late. I persevered and the articles started to appear. I saw scope for all types of subject, from a series on old bottles for a winemaking magazine, to a piece on historic horseshoes for a treasure hunting monthly, and several pieces on world coins, with wildlife reverses.

I started to produce articles about some of the birds and animals which passed through our hands. People wanted to read about them and, more importantly, they were relieved that at last somebody would take on the responsibility of this particular bird or that mammal. Charlie Norris became a regular visitor with the local casualties. We received many late night visits from police cars, usually bringing a tawny owl road casualty, and always willing to accept a cup of coffee. Fortunately, the urgent call from Aylesbury police station about a renegade kestrel came at a more humane time for us, one mid-morning.

The Fleet family had lived for many years without incident at Bierton, a small village soon to be embroiled in Aylesbury's urban

A bird in the hand

By Les Stocker

...the mild weather, earlier this year, has assisted the wild birds in their efforts to make up the numbers, lost in last year's hard winter. Our local gardens and woods are once again ringing with the frantic calls of adult birds shepherding their awkward youngsters to safe places of refuge.

Most altricial young birds (i.e. those born naked and helpless) leave the nest before being capable of fending for themselves. In fact this takes time away from the parents use this time away from the nest to teach the youngsters how and where to find food and generally how to survive the rigours of a wild existence. This system has worked for thousands of years but now it is being interfered with by the misguided helpfulness of some people. In spite of the extensive publicity, condemning any interference, many people still assume that any young flightless bird, is destitute and an orphan. They invariably, with the best of intentions, take it to a supposedly better situation. Meanwhile the parent birds have probably returned to feed their youngster, who is now nowhere to be found. They naturally assume that it has been taken by one of the many predators and after a short search abandon any further ideas of looking after the fledgling.

...is far more capable of the task than we, and a far more competent teacher of the ways of the bird world.

On being called to a young bird, we endeavour to trace where it was found. We return it to that site and watch at a discreet distance still searching for their fledgling. Happily in many cases the families are reunited but some fledglings have to be recaptured and cared for during the weeks until they are fully grown. This requires a lot of patience and dedication together with expertise in persuading young birds to fend for themselves.

This precaution ensures that any predator has less chance of destroying all the brood.

The appearance of a predator near the nest will sometimes cause the nestlings to flee in all directions, once again saving some of the family from disaster.

The commonest cause of leaving the nest, before completely intended, is completely accidental. In growing and then exercising their newly formed limbs and muscles, young birds sometimes overbalance and fall from the nest, unable to return or call...

Complications

Added complications occur with birds that exist on live food. They have to be taught to hunt and cannot be released to the wild without this ability. When they are set free, food has to be left out in case they cannot manage to catch their own. Owls are notorious for leaving their nests before they can fly properly and we are left...

Misinformed

Our own bird rescue centre is, as usual, been inundated with calls from misinundated people who have 'saved' mums and deliver... from knowing...

Photo: Eric Husking

Henry flies into trouble

WATERLOGGED and exhausted, Henry the heron was fished out of Aylesbury canal two weeks ago probably thinking his last moment had come.

But the big bird found he was in good hands for the early morning anglers Gavin and the RSPCA Inspector, Mr Charles Morris who took him to Aylesbury's Wildlife Hospital...

Above: The ground beetle (seen here greatly enlarged) is the jaws of the cabbage patch

RSPCA Inspector Mr Charles North gives Henry a helping hand as the heron prepares for lift off.

Last Friday, Les and Inspector Morris gave Henry a clean bill of health and set him free on the canal banks.

---

is tiful

---

fast, the superb Stocker on a six- ...nd

...you turned over ...leaves and dis- ...ed to get

...ng 31 October 1981

IT'S LEGS AND CO!

Centipedes may look like an armoured menace, but they make fine allies in the vegetable patch and flower bed. Les Stocker stands up for a leggy pest-controller

...pede, the lithobius,

...the legs. Its flexible jointed body allows it to travel across all types of uneven terrain, a fair...

...gardener's ...ing beneficial ...pests is that ...lly move at ...plant-eating ...snail's pace, ...green stuff

Scolioplanes, another hunter of garden pests, grows to 3in.

...tipedes have only seven pairs of legs. They get the full adult total of 15 pairs only after considerable growth and four skin changes. Taking three years to mature, they then live and breed for a further 2–3 years, and the amount of garden pests they eat in that...

...mites; slugs and their eggs; caterpillars; insects; a few...

...another. The result was a number of small snakes in one place at one time, causing the farmer to panic and take the destructive action.

Once the crisis was over, I attempted to explain, to the farmer and his men, the futility of their actions in destroying many beautiful and harmless grass snakes.

Grass snake

It is a popular misconception that all snakes are villains and are best destroyed before they can deal their deadly blows to all who look upon them. Nothing can be further from the truth; the harmless grass snake is the model of good behaviour to all except his prey which is predominantly frogs, toads, newts, fish and some small rodents.

The grass snake is the largest of the British snakes averaging 70–90 cm in length, although one specimen captured, some time ago, was 175 cm long. A real monster, many would say, but still completely harmless to man and his property and probably very useful in disposing of the occasional rat or mouse.

The female grass snake is larger than the male. Older females will lay up to 40 eggs, but the number is usually between 10 and 20, during June or July, in a pile of rotting vegetation where the heat generated will assist in the incubation.

Although a grass snake prefers to feed on cold blooded creatures, its contemporary, the much maligned adder, will consume many of the small harmful rodents that can be such a nuisance.

The adder is altogether a much sho...

...less than 10 people have died from its bite in the last fifty years.

The adder is a very shy creature and will quickly disappear into cover if it detects the approach of a human being. Should it be accidentally disturbed and startled, it may attempt to bite but, as it has only a very small mouth, it would only be able to clasp small objects such as fingers or toes. Most bites have been incurred by inadvertently treading, with unprotected feet, on adders hidden in long grass and undergrowth.

Should the unexpected happen, and somebody get bitten, there is no need to 'cut out the poison' as was the practice in most Western films; in fact this remedy is fraught with danger, not from any venom but from infection from unsterilized blades and bandages. The victim of an adder bite should be kept quiet and have pressure applied to slow the carriage of the venom by the bloodstream. The nearest hospital will soon administer anti-toxin and put matters right.

Folklore decrees that adders and all snakes are lethal and should be destroyed without compunction. Most people do not realise the tremendous amount of good work that snakes perform. Apart from the obvious benefit, of disposing of harmful rodents, they practise the laws of evolution and effectively cull the sickly and weak specimens of other reptiles and amphibians.

Adder

Simple recognition of the different species would, I'm sure, alleviate a lot of the needless killings, especially of the non-poisonous snakes. If people are afraid of the venomous adder, then they...

CAGE & AVIARY BIRDS

Squire — a lord of the

THE LAPWING (*Vanellus vanellus*), like the Curlew, is well known as a bird of open spaces and haunting calls. Often known as the Peewit, after its call, it is increasingly seen in distant fields, either feeding, displaying or protecting its young (writes Les Stocker).

However, I was surprised to answer the door one morning to a bright-faced youngster offering up what was obviously a badly injured Lapwing. I thanked the young lad and gave him a packet of sweets.

Luckily, the injured bird did not appear to be bleeding and, after a warm drink of glucose and water, it was placed in a box, so that it could rest and overcome the shock it had experienced.

The following morning found a much perkier invalid strutting around, pecking at all likely looking morsels on the kitchen floor.

I prepared a meal of cleaned earthworms, gentles and a few mealworms. The food was obviously to his satisfaction, as no sooner had he cleared the dish than he started to preen and re-adjust his dishevelled plumage.

When he had settled again, I felt it an opportune moment to examine the damaged wing. Inspection confirmed my fears. The wing was, indeed, broken – a clean break of the humerus, which was probably the result of being hit by a car.

I clipped his damaged feathers away, joined the broken bone sections and fixed them firmly in place with a strong, lightweight cardboard splint.

This in turn was supported by straps of zinc-oxide plaster around the body, which were nearly affixed, taking care not to impair the movement of the undamaged wing and legs.

Throughout the next three weeks "Squire", as he was christened, was allowed the freedom of the garden, strutting around like a lord of the manor. He was far more adept at finding wireworms, insects, earthworms and leatherjackets than I could ever be.

Perhaps his most endearing habit was to stand completely still, moving only his right leg in a shuffling movement.

Tasty morsel

This is also a common practice with Black-headed Gulls, but how does Squire search for food...

'Squire's greatest... and sprint around... to all the magnit...

...wing. There were... patches, but these w... replaced at the la... moult.

Now that he w... both wings, albeit... had to be confined... (5.4m) long × 6f... 6ft (1.8m) high, r... and he w...

sprawl, when all of a sudden, as eleven-year-old Giles was going down the garden to collect his bike, a bird of prey swooped out of the sky and scratched him just below his eye. Elder sister, Louise, was also attacked about the legs, and Mrs Fleet had the bird's talons embedded in her head. Visions of Alfred Hitchcock's *Birds* sprang to their minds so they phoned the police, which is where we came in.

I had my own theories on the reasons for the attacks, but took along large nets and thick gloves just in case. It sounded to me like a tamed kestrel that had escaped or else had been irresponsibly released. Being tame it would have been quite inexperienced in the art of hunting and would be looking to the Fleet family to provide food. It had, in fact, been trying to land on each of them, but in their mutual panic had only managed to catch them with its razor-sharp talons before flying off again. It had probably been raised in captivity on a diet of day-old male chicks. Perhaps I had better explain that in chicken-rearing establishments all male chicks are humanely killed as soon as they hatch. I can't do anything to change this practice and, like all other people looking after animals, I make use of these cullings which would otherwise go to waste.

Taking a defrosting day-old chick in a gloved hand, I ventured out into the attack zone. No sign of the aggressor. At the bottom of the garden were large fields surrounded by English hedgerow interspersed with mature elms and oaks. If the kestrel were there it could see me, whereas I had no chance of spotting it amongst the leaves and branches. I waved the chick in the air and she came like a rocket across the fields. Swooping about four feet off the ground, she flew up at the last moment and landed on a gatepost just by my outstretched hand. She grabbed the chick and I grabbed her. I was a hero – but she *was* tame and, in no time at all (and safely tied now), she had made friends with Giles and Louise and was sitting on the boy's gloved hand. Obviously, I could never release her. The same thing would only have happened all over again somewhere else. She would have to live in our growing collection of aviaries. At least until I could find a captive breeding programme for her to go into.

She turned out to be one of the friendliest birds I have ever known, showing great delight in having her feathers stroked or her chest

The kestrel was used to sitting quietly on somebody's fist.

Food chart for baby birds

Defrosted Frozen Mice or Day-old Chicks	Chick Crumbs and Fresh Water	Complan and Porridge Oats	WHT Glop
Hawks Owls Falcons Gulls Corvids	Ducks Geese Swans	Pigeons Doves	Passerines (garden birds) Corvids (crows, etc) Hirundines (swallows, martins, etc)
	Sprats + Thiamine Supplement	Whitebait + Thiamine Supplement	Small Clean White Maggots, Pinkies or Mealworms
	Seabirds Herons	Grebes Kingfishers Small Fish-eaters	Moorhens Coots Insectivores

All frozen products must be defrosted before being offered

tickled – an exceptional bird, obviously used to sitting quietly on somebody's fist.

Shortly after her arrival we received an unusual cry for help from a young theatre group in Watford. The Watford Palace Theatre for Youth were staging that renowned social study *Kes* written by Barry Hines and Allan Stronach, but the kestrel, a male, which was to have played the title role had escaped from its owner only days before the first night. Could we help? At the time I was unaware of the problems to do with kestrel nest-robbing which the film of *Kes* had provoked and, as I was all in favour of supporting youth projects of that type, I agreed to help, bearing in mind that our latest kestrel was completely at ease being handled.

Ian Tuersley, who was to play Billy Casper, called into Aylesbury to introduce himself to his possible co-star and struck up an immediate rapport with the bird. She stood firm and quiet on his fist, but there was no way of knowing whether she would be as quiet in front of the footlights and the audience, or whether she would scream and flap and ruin the months of hard work which the youngsters had put

into their production? The only way to find out was at the full dress rehearsal in the theatre.

With fingers crossed, I carried her into the darkened theatre and, sitting in the front stalls, judged her reactions to the ever-changing lights and sometimes boisterous and noisy scenes in the production. She stood there like a trouper, bobbing her head knowingly and taking in every word and movement in front of her. Then came the moment of her entrance. I made my way backstage ready to hand her, the glove and other paraphernalia to Billy Casper as he reached into the wings. We had rehearsed the changeover but suddenly I found myself standing with the bird at one exit while Ian was expecting us at another. We soon overcame that hiccup and she saw the footlights for the first time from the other side.

Standing on Ian's fist she looked about, shrugged and ignored the diversions and settled to her part without much ado. She even ad-libbed at the right moments, especially when Billy's schoolmaster, played by Simon Chambers, came too close, exactly as described in Barry Hines' book. She was supreme, really earning the feast I offered her afterwards. Fine so far, but the real hurdle was fast approaching, with the first performance that evening.

The auditorium was packed as I waited tremulously in the wings. The kestrel cocked an ear at the applause for the earlier scenes but ignored other diversions as she tidied any feathers that were out of place. Then came our cue. The stage manager beckoned as Billy came out calling, 'Kes, Kes,' and then, smoothly, she was out there.

A muted gasp of wonder came from the audience. She must have picked up the admiration for she stood proud as an eagle. Ian and Simon played their parts superbly yet I imagine they felt some truth in the old adage that animals are notorious scene-stealers. Then, in a flash, it was over, she came off to rapturous applause and a reward of prime meat: she had earned it.

She gave three more performances and then returned to the peace and quiet and the battered male kestrel who had become her beau during their few weeks in our aviary.

I now have my reservations about the whole incident, because of what I learned later about the effects of the film, but the kestrel suffered no harm whatsoever and she did save the play which was of such importance to that young theatre group.

★

We had to come to know Watford and its people quite well, so it came as no surprise when we were asked if we would like to set up a fundraising stall at the Oxhey Village Fête to be held just on the outskirts. Until then we had always scraped together the money to feed and house the animals and birds from our meagre resources but the fête was a chance to ease the situation.

Pulling out all the stops, Sue and I started to collect together all manner of bric-à-brac, jumble, old books, in fact anything saleable. Anyone who brought in a casualty, in the inevitable cardboard box, was given in return a small pile of tickets requesting likely articles.

Eventually when the great day came we had a substantial amount of material and, with a stall made out of paste tables and an old tarpaulin, we were soon set up and ready for business. At that moment the heavens opened and one by one the other stalls packed up and went home. Even the fairground whirligig droned to a halt

There was nearly always a tawny owl in the garage.

and gave up. Meanwhile the tarpaulin let us into its little secret – it was full of holes. Undaunted, we tactically positioned under the drips any of our objets d'art which could hold water, but every now and then one drop would find the gap at the back of my collar, sending a rivulet of icy water down the spine. Many visitors to the fête had braved the weather and, finding us the only stall standing, if somewhat bedraggled, came to shelter under our dripping tarpaulin and started spending money.

We did a very brisk trade in soggy goods and soggy pound notes, but had soon amassed ninety pounds towards our bird fund. We did not have many patients then, so that little windfall, or should I say rainfall, would support them for quite some time.

During that summer we had another two stalls at village fêtes, both in brilliant sunshine, and our bird fund began to look healthy. We ran our next stall in Milton Keynes market just before Christmas, and had to light the bric-à-brac candles to keep our hands warm. But it was worth it: we felt we had enough money to carry the birds through the winter.

Christmas Day saw a robin casualty arrive with a very poorly barn owl. We were due to visit my parents in London on Boxing Day and, although I felt confident about leaving the robin in a warm cage, with a nice dish of lukewarm maggots, the barn owl was causing me great concern and would have to travel with us.

All the family were there – aunts, uncles, cousins I had not seen for years – but I spent all day in the bathroom with my barn owl, trying to keep him alive. I know it's not good Christmas reading, but he was suffering from a complete blockage of his excretory system by a large, solid ball of urates and faeces. At that time I knew nothing about the condition or how to cure it; I knew only that I had to try and clear it before it killed him. Hour after hour I gently bathed him with warm water, clipping away ever so slowly at that solid mass. I did manage to clear some of it but I felt so guilty about commandeering the bathroom while others were trying to enjoy Christmas that we decided to leave early so as to give him peace and quiet at home.

He was still alive when we got back but obviously was not going to make it, so, rather than subject him to further treatment, I let him die peacefully on a soft towel in front of the electric fire in our lounge. That was a miserable Christmas, but the following day a new character came into our lives, lifting the gloom and putting a new slant on the meaning of improvisation.

There he was, a tiny bird, about the size of a small pigeon, with enormous feet almost as long as his body – a little grebe out of water. He had been caught out by the freezing weather and, not being able to find any ice-free water, had taken up temporary residence in a pool of bathwater which could not drain away because the drain below it had frozen. The lady who found him had looked out of her window after unplugging her bath and spotted him happily (little grebes always seem to look happy) paddling across the newly formed steaming pond.

It's important to keep water birds in their national environment otherwise their feathers seem to become very dry and they sink at the first opportunity. All our outside water containers froze as soon as they were filled, so this 'Donald Duck' of a bird had to make do with living, for the time being, in our bath, with enough space to torpedo up and down, perhaps hoping to find a fish or two. Whitebait seemed a likely answer to his dietary requirements but he completely ignored

The little grebe in the bath.

those we dropped in. Possibly the strange enamel bottom of his unusual pool was distracting him. We would have to find alternative accommodation when the shops opened after the Christmas break.

My solution was a medium-sized aquarium with a generous layer of gravel looking something like the bed of a stream. Once in the aquarium he loved the new-found depth of water, expertly diving to investigate every corner, those enormous feet propelling him through the water. The silver air bubbles trapped in his plumage added to his streamlined appearance, keeping him thoroughly dry so that, when he surfaced, he still bobbed like a cork with his feet frantically treading water as he sailed around the tank. We tried the whitebait again but, although he followed each of them to the bottom, his penchant was obviously for live fish not the frozen substitute.

Not too difficult a problem, until you remember that every stream or pool in the locality was a solid mass of ice and people were actually walking on the canal. There was just one place that might still be free running. At Marsworth between the Grand Union Canal and Star-tops Reservoir is a pipe which emerges from the bank and seems to be some kind of overflow system between the two. It was still running, keeping open a hole in the frozen pool below. Summoning up all my childhood experience of netting for tiddlers on Clapham Common I managed to catch a few sticklebacks to put in my jam jar and the grebe was soon showing his prowess at out-swimming the unfortunate fish. While I was out fishing under the drainpipe at Marsworth a perplexed passer-by told me of a section of the River Thame, below a weir, which usually remained free of ice throughout the winter. It sounded an ideal place to fish but, better still, it was an ideal place to release our visitor, if only to put an end to my infantile fishing expeditions.

The grebe had no sooner touched the water than he dived and disappeared for ages, only to reappear bobbing to the surface twenty yards away, revelling in his element. Then he was under once more, down into his own wild underworld. A happy ending to the story, but it's worth remembering that freezing weather can sometimes have disastrous effects on water birds.

Whenever the canals and reservoirs are frozen we receive innumerable calls reporting birds 'stuck' in the ice. After a few dozen of these false alarms, where the birds invariably wandered off, we learnt to ask the caller to return to the scene just to make sure. One February night, however, the caller was our RSPCA Inspector who, like us, would have been familiar with any false alarms. The birds in peril were three black-headed gulls which had apparently been shot and left to die on the ice covering a reservoir near Abingdon in Oxfordshire. I went out with Charlie to look at the situation and, sure enough, there were three birds about twenty yards offshore, lying on ice that was far too thin to bear the weight of any rescue attempt. Reluctantly, we had to return to Aylesbury to consider a possible rescue the following morning.

But I could not sleep. The thought of those birds lying there suffering in sub-zero temperatures was just too much for my conscience. Dragging Sue and Colin out of bed, I decided on a plan that was perhaps foolhardy, but as I saw it my intervention was the only chance those birds had.

We had an old inflatable boat, which was down more than it was up, and this was to be my means of getting out to the birds without, I hoped, disappearing under the ice. So, armed with the boat, an old rope and a flask of coffee, the three of us set out to drive the forty miles to Abingdon.

The temperature was six degrees below freezing, but we were well wrapped. The reservoir itself was lit by the streetlamps of a nearby main road so we could see our three casualties and in the distance, about sixty yards out, the other gulls and waterfowl which had found an unfrozen stretch of water on which to roost. Flopping the boat off the top of the car we pumped in some more air and tied the rope to the stern. Sue and Colin were to hold onto the rope and pull me in if I floated into difficulties. Breaking a circle of ice, we launched the boat. Then, by hanging over the prow, I could break the ice ahead with a paddle and slowly, inch by inch, row my way towards the gulls. Actually, the boat did not feel insecure even though it was losing air all the way. The birds looked horrifyingly still. Sue shouted that the rope had run out but I was almost there and reasonably confident that I could get back, so I told her to let go. Another ten feet of ice-breaking and I was at the nearest gull which was already dead. There was no movement from the other two but I pressed on. Both were dead. Then the 'if only's' started: 'if only we had come out earlier', 'if only we had received the call during the day'. It was no good: deep down I knew that we had tried our best.

Then I had to get back to dry land before the boat finally wheezed its last. The channel I had hacked through the ice had stayed open and rowing back was much less of an effort. Silently we loaded the boat back on the roofrack, tied it on, drank the coffee and started the icy drive back to Aylesbury, full of gloom and despondency.

We were struggling to survive financially, putting all our waking hours into wildlife and yet incidents like this still cropped up and kicked us in the teeth. Was it all worth it? Was it really worth avidly collecting all the special offer tokens we could muster and then running the gauntlet of the Sainsbury check-out girls as we offered the tokens to pay for our grocery bills? Marks & Spencer was definitely off limits. We never went out for a meal. Every post brought a demand for money for this or for that. But a good night's sleep would help and a quick tour of the thriving patients in the morning soon put things back in perspective.

I decided that at last I would have to execute the deed which I had dreaded and postponed. After all, actors do it when they are 'resting' and in this age of redundancies it was becoming the accepted norm. I went and signed on at the Job Centre. Coming away clutching my UB40, I sensed a weight had been taken off my mind but, every ensuing fortnight as I queued to sign my docket, I felt like an outcast. In fact, if the queue stretched out into the street, I would drive around until I could join it out of the public gaze. You feel less than human, dreading the cold-hearted comments of the clerks and living in fear of being summoned to see one of the supervisors. There was only ever one friendly face behind the bench, a tall, genial Scotsman with a silver fish earring. Quite out of place in that morgue, he made a visit seem less harrowing, but when Fish left to front the pop group, Marillion, it was back to the same inquisition for me – a hell that I just had to get away from.

Foxes and Boxes

It was amazing how quickly that fortnightly sign-on day came around. No sooner had you run the gauntlet of the public gaze, the complacent clerk and the inquisitional supervisor than, it seemed, you had to go through it all over again. Without it we could probably have eked out a fairly frugal existence, but the birds were costing us more and more. We had tried the property market, all to no avail; we wondered whether we should approach the owners of land or properties that might welcome the potential of a wildlife rescue centre, with its spin offs into conservation and education.

Then bingo! An opportunity arose in the first week of our enquiries. The Greater London Council, fast becoming almost infamous for its community projects and conservation work, was developing the area of south-east London just above the Thames Barrier and had a vacant site that might just prove suitable to get us off the dole queue. The district was a major housing and development showpiece known as Thamesmead. I had been there many years before in the early days of building up our domestic engineering business when I would spend days 'on the road', learning all the techniques and pitfalls my engineers would have to face. It had struck me then as an architectural nightmare: masses of concrete and

ACTION

Basic first aid kit
Small animals and birds

- Forceps and artery forceps
- Scissors
- Small torch
- Savlon – for bathing wounds
- Cotton wool
- Dermisol Multi-cleanse solution
- 19g sterile needle (to cure abscesses and subcutaneous emphysema)
- Ceruvet for maggots in ears
- Optrex for eyes
- Vetwrap self-adhesive bandage
- Bamboo for cutting up to make splints
- Cotton buds
- Lightweight leather gloves (for handling hedgehogs and birds of prey)
- Elastic bands for restraining corvid beaks
- Zinc oxide plaster tape (½ inch)
- Chloramphenicol eye ointment

piazzas infiltrated by tunnels and pathways lined with anonymous 'little box' houses and flats tenanted by refugees of the massive re-constitution of London's heartland.

We found it had changed little, only that those bland concrete walls and pillars were festooned with spray-paint graffiti, the slim hand-picked cherry trees had long since been ripped out leaving little hexagonal patches of bare soil and chewing gum wrappers amongst the flagstones. Every roadway had its own burnt-out car and pram chassis while the whole conglomeration was overshadowed and overpowered by a constantly humming motorway flyover.

I wanted to turn back without even looking, but pulled up by the remains of a brook just to see if there was any life left in the area. Hearing a tap on the window I looked across to see an elderly lady, attracted to the 'We Save Wildlife' logo on the side of our car.

'Have you come about the swans?'

I had not seen any swans, but asked her what the problem was.

'The kids have been stoning them again, so I phoned the Council. I thought you were them.'

I explained why we were there but assured her that if I saw the swans I would check to make sure they weren't injured. She seemed aghast at the idea that anybody might want to move to Thamesmead.

'You don't want to move here. It's a dreadful place. I used to live in a small house in Peckham, but then the Council pulled it down and moved me out here. I don't know anyone, nobody wants to know me and I have to have three locks on my door to keep the hooligans out.'

'We used to have a city farm over there,' pointing in the direction of our proposed site, 'But the kids got in one night and pulled the heads off the chickens. I'll spend the rest of my days here, but the Council don't care. Whatever you do, don't come to this place.'

I wanted to say, 'Why don't you do this or that, or come and live with us in Aylesbury?' But I knew my suggestions would be impossible. I could do nothing to help the poor lady and, after her descriptions of the place, I knew that we would have to decline the G L C's offer.

I can still feel the relief as we drove west, out of London, back to the sanity of Aylesbury, but can also still hear the desperation of that old lady and wonder how many more there are, just like her, the victims of unthinking town planners.

★

Being more and more involved with animals and birds and taking in a continual stream of casualties, I was becoming used but never immune to the inhumanity of some people and was not too surprised to hear of the cruelty of those swan-stoning kids – we had already met so many cases of malicious or ignorant callousness, though not usually perpetrated by the younger generation who are, on the whole, considerate of the feelings of wildlife.

The most horrifying, and enough to break your heart, was the sight of a proud kestrel grovelling on the ground quite unable to walk, stand, preen or do anything for itself. Brought to me by a young lad from Cheddington, a village near to Tring, the bird had obviously been in this state for some while and was by then a mass of broken feathers contaminated by its own faeces as it had spun round and round, using its battered wings as its only way of manoeuvring. The boy was in tears. He had bought the kestrel from an obviously unscrupulous dealer when it was only three days old. He had had no idea how to look after it but had diligently fed it on a diet of raw beef cut meticulously into bite-size pieces. He could not understand why the bird had become weaker and weaker; in desperation he had finally found a vet who, knowing of my involvement with birds of prey, had suggested he contact me.

Enough to break your heart – a malnourished kestrel.

An x-ray of the bird showed the horrifying consequences of its meat-only diet. It had little or no bone structure and where there were bones, particularly in the legs, they had spontaneously fractured, making it impossible for the bird to stand and keep itself clean. It was suffering from a probably irreversible deficiency of calcium and other elements in its diet. Birds of prey should be fed only on whole dead animals, be they specially prepared mice or day-old chicks. Quite apart from the minerals in this type of natural food, the birds also need to swallow quantities of fur and feathers in order to produce the pellets necessary to keep their digestion (and consequently general demeanour) in tip-top condition. The dealer who had sold the bird should have made sure that the young boy knew which food to give the kestrel, how to house it and perhaps most difficult of all, how to raise it from a three-day-old helpless chick to a fully fledged adult. Even then, should he have sold a potentially dangerous bird to a young boy? When the Wildlife Countryside Act came into force in 1981, offering more protection to Britain's falcons and hawks, I had hoped that the trade in kestrels would be controlled but looking through the advertisements in bird papers I can imagine that there are still three-day-old chicks being sold to gullible youngsters.

For two days I deliberated over the fate of this poor kestrel. But I knew it was hopeless: she would have to be humanely destroyed by the vet. Then fate took a hand and she died over the second night, a blessed release from the torture which her whole life had been in the hands of man.

I now realise that it's only a few people who really do not have any feelings towards animals and birds, but at that time every other call seemed to involve me with man's inhumanity to other creatures. I had a call from a distraught lady who was living in a caravan on the site where her house was being built. A pigeon had been injured on the site and as she had no form of transport (she lived in a village about fifteen miles from Aylesbury) she asked if I would go and collect it.

Eventually, having found the site, hidden as it was behind a row of bungalows, I parked amongst the rubble only to be greeted with cat

Myrtle would have to spend up to 3 weeks suspended.

calls of 'Why bother with a bleedin' pigeon?' 'If it were me, I'd wring its bloody neck.' 'There's too many pigeons around 'ere. Bang it on the 'ead.'

Some louts working on the site had obviously been having a great time at the expense of the pigeon: no wonder the distraught lady in the caravan greeted me with tears in her eyes. Putting her mind at rest, I wrapped the pigeon, which had apparently broken both legs, in a towel and went out to face the onslaught once more. Another tirade of chiacking, but I had heard enough by then, and, marching up to the loudest mouth, offered him the pigeon and said, daring him, 'Go on then, you wring its neck.' With his audience looking sheepish and shifty, he knew he had lost his support and could manage only a whimpered, 'I didn't really mean it.' I felt distinctly shaky but refused to let them see that as I drove off their site, foot to the floor and wheels spinning. I even lit my cigarette before I had put on my seat belt.

I was getting used to finding birds, usually pigeons, with both their legs broken, but I still do not know how they manage to do it. Perhaps they catch them on overhead wires. By using a traction cradle I had specially designed for that type of injury, we have successfully treated herons, ducks, greenfinches and blackbirds. This pigeon – Myrtle, we called her – would have to spend up to three weeks suspended above the base of the cradle, to prevent her from putting any pressure on the broken legs while they healed.

She soon recovered and, after a spell of physiotherapy, she learnt to walk again and was soon out amongst the pigeons being released from our garden. Like all the others she stayed around for two weeks and then flew off, perhaps, as pigeons are remarkably loyal to their spouses, to join a mate.

Although we were then taking in an increasing number of species of wild bird we had little contact with British mammals, except for the occasional wood mouse, vole or shrew caught by people's cats. All the books I had acquired dealt with bird casualties with never a mention of anything with four legs. So, when our first fox arrived, I had to try to look as if I knew what I was doing. I decided to put the fox into the garage for the time being.

Releasing the fox on Wimbledon Common.

The fox had been rescued from a gypsy encampment and looked remarkably healthy as he glared at me from the top of an old wardrobe. His yellow eyes darted at me, then into the corner for an escape route, then back to me. He did not miss a thing. His mouth hung slightly open, showing sharp teeth. His jaws were not like a dog's, as I had imagined, but were long and very thin and those teeth seemed so much more lethal. I had always been told that foxes were dirty, but the bright red coat and white chest glowed from constant grooming. This was a truly wild animal, a masterpiece of natural perfection which I, for one, was not going to approach just then. Instead, I left him a bowl of water and some dog food and came out and hurriedly shut the door. He was safe in the garage for the moment.

Everything seemed to be happening at once. In addition to the fox, we also had an extremely large terrapin which had been hooked by an angler on the canal, and an enormous Indian python which had been rescued from one of those people who imagine that keeping a large snake incarcerated in their living room will improve their macho image. To make matters worse, this owner had taken great delight in entertaining guests by putting live white mice in with the snake and applauding their demise.

There is an unfortunate misconception amongst reptile keepers that snakes will take only live food, usually a poor unsuspecting white mouse. I think snakes are marvellous creatures, but always chuckle at the David and Goliath story of how a white mouse was once put in a vivarium with a sleeping python. Uninterrupted by the slumbering giant, the mouse, true to mouse tradition, had started to nibble anything which even vaguely resembled food, including the python. Striking it lucky, it somehow managed to nibble into a vital part of the snake's anatomy, killing it in the process. Imagine the keeper's surprise when he returned to gloat over his prize python.

Of course this is an occurrence in a million, but the point is that the whole nasty procedure is totally unnecessary. Apart from being 'cruelly terrifying' to the mouse, as defined by the Protection of Animals Act 1911, it can also be highly offensive to visitors, a point many zoos would do well to note.

So, although this particular python was used to taking live food, I intended to feed him only on dead food – a good test of my theory. I decided to try using a defrosted and warmed-up day-old chick.

The snake showed no interest whatsoever in one or two dead chicks lying around the bottom of its tank. I obviously had to simulate a live bird before there was any hope of a reaction. Tying a piece of string loosely around the chick I dangled it in front of the snake's nose. I slid it up and down its flanks. I even tried the sudden spurt escape trick which sometimes stimulates predators to strike. Still nothing. For over half an hour I wiggled that chick on the piece of string then, as I touched the snake's flanks for the umpteenth time,

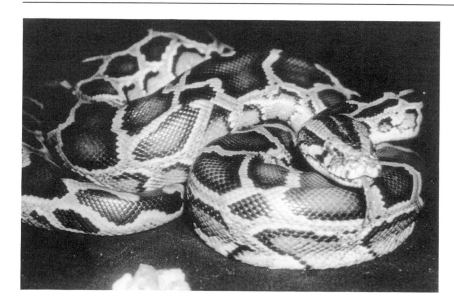

An absolutely enormous Indian python.

he struck. Like lightning his jaws opened and clamped on the chick and the string. In great gulps he started to swallow and I had visions of him taking in the string as well, with me still attached. My patented slip knot did not work so, very tentatively, reaching almost into the snake's jaws, I unpicked the string and pulled it free as the chick disappeared from view. It took me nearly a whole morning to get a decent meal into him, but at least I had proved that it could be done.

Exotic reptiles like the python and the terrapin need very special-ised treatment and housing and for the next two days Sue phoned well-known reptile keepers just in case one of them had room for two more responsibilities. There were many who would take only the python but it was more of a struggle to place both at the same time. Eventually a reptile centre in West London agreed to take them both into their collection.

We couldn't make the trip for another two days, but we could take the opportunity to release the fox and a fully fit wood pigeon at the same time on one of the large London commons where they would be safe from hunting or shooting.

Meanwhile, the fox had taken over the garage. If you ever want anything demolished, get yourself a fox. We had left him overnight in the garage until I could rig up alternative accommodation the following day. As I very carefully opened the door in the morning, a vista of complete devastation hit me: here were tins of paint, off the shelves, mixed with boxes of screws, nails and daffodil bulbs. Packets of bird seed had burst open among the spilled bottles of home-made wine and everything cloth or leather, including my best climbing boots, had been either chewed or torn to shreds. Nothing was left standing or on the shelves: there was just a mountain of chaos in the middle of the floor with one very handsome, exhausted fox curled up on top of it all. Once more I left quickly, closed the door and tried to think of a secure way of housing him until the following day. I could find no solution: he would have to stay in the garage after all. He could not possibly cause any more damage – I hoped.

We then had four animals to take to London, so, planning to combine the trip with a visit to my parents, the next day I loaded the four cardboard boxes together with Sue, Colin and Poppy into the car and off we went.

Over my shoulder as I drove towards the M4, I could hear all manner of frantic scratchings coming from the back but I could see nothing in my rear-view mirror and Colin was checking the boxes at intervals. All went well until we swung onto the motorway. 'Dad, the fox is out,' cried Colin. Looking in the mirror I saw the fox staring back at me and could see a pigeon frantically trying to fly through the side window. Pulling onto the hard shoulder I made Colin come into the front with Sue and Poppy while I went round the back to investigate. The fox had not only successfully chewed out of his cardboard box but he had also managed to release the crazy pigeon and the python which was trying to disappear under the rear seat. I dared not open the tailgate as I could just imagine the disaster if all of a sudden, in the middle of the day, a fox were to run through the motorway traffic. I went back to the front of the car again and climbed in over Colin to get at the problem from the inside. The pigeon was going berserk, scattering feathers everywhere as it tried to get out. There was no sign of the snake but the fox was trying to break out of the rear window, luckily offering the back of his head in my direction. He did not have a chance to move as I made a desperate dive and lunge to grab his scruff. We ended up in a heap on top of the remains of the boxes but I held firmly to his neck. Great, I was parked on a motorway, holding a fox but with nothing to put him in. I could not possibly drive all the way to Wimbledon with him in one hand and the steering wheel in the other. Then Colin came up with the answer: 'Why not put Poppy's collar and lead on him and tie him to something?' Brilliant idea, we agreed, and, as I always carried an enormously heavy tool box which even I could hardly move, I was sure that, tied to it, the fox would be secure until we reached the release site. Sue had managed to catch the pigeon and opened the tailgate so that I could fall out, still clutching the fox. Colin had hold of Poppy and passed me her collar and lead which fitted the fox who was not much bigger than she. I put the pigeon in with the terrapin and, having unwound the snake from the back seat, stuffed it unceremoniously into a ramshackle box I had made out of all the other bits of cardboard. Now to continue the journey.

We were to pass the reptile delivery point first so decided to deliver the python and terrapin before anything else went wrong. We didn't even have time for a quick look around but, when handing over our two reptiles, I saw spacious enclosures containing other pythons and a large pool for the terrapin – they were going to live in luxury from then on.

On to the common. The wood pigeon was gone in an instant, cracking his wings as he went and showering us with a few more feathers. I knew a fenced-in copse where I could let the fox go but, even then, as I unbuckled the collar, he had a good try at biting me before melting away into the undergrowth.

I needed a good stiff whisky by the time we got to my parents after one of the most traumatic car journeys even we are likely to have.

On the way home we discussed the possibility of another fox casualty being brought in and how we could house it. However, for the moment all our casualties seemed to be birds and, with our vet's advocacy of the use of subcutaneous fluids, we were able to get most of them through the initial twenty-four hours of severe shock which

kills most avian patients. Having improved our success rate by an enormous percentage it was becoming important to know how the birds fared once they were released.

Luckily, I met one of the foremost experts on bird-ringing on my first excursion into the archives of the Ornithological Department of the British Museum Natural History Section based at Tring, only a few miles from Aylesbury. I had gone there to investigate the remains of a bird's wing which I had extricated from a hole in the chest of a sparrowhawk. The sparrowhawk was recovering perfectly, but it intrigued me how a part of another bird's wing came to be embedded in its chest. My appointment was with Graham Cowell, keeper of the bird skeleton collection at the Museum. After dissection of the wing under the microscope and comparison with numerous bones of small birds, we finally established that it was off a house martin's wing, but we could only surmise how it got there. It was while we were discussing our hypotheses that Dr Philip Burton came in and joined in the conversation. Despite being dressed in jeans and a Dallas-type belt with an owl on the buckle, Philip's attitude was that of the typical professor, completely engrossed in his work and his birds. Not only was he the country's foremost anatomist but he was also a leading light in the field of bird-ringing and he volunteered, there and then, to ring any of our birds ready for release. Being very much a field ornithologist, he was also able to advise me of suitable release areas and techniques – and, incidentally, after a pint of beer he played terrific boogie-woogie piano. He called at the hospital on a fairly regular basis, his car often bedecked by long ladders, each with all kinds of coloured garments flying off the ends. Mind you, the absent-minded professor invariably showed through, as he always went to the house next door before realising his mistake. Forever in a hurry, scurrying from one appointment to the next, he always found time to come and ring a bird or help to identify the oddities which were starting to turn up at the hospital.

On his visits that summer he told us of a farmer who had phoned him from Steeple Claydon, a village north of Aylesbury, with tales of a pair of merlins nesting in one of his fields. Now, we all know that this dashing little falcon, a bird of the high moors of Wales and

Scotland, could never be found in Buckinghamshire, not even on passage let alone nesting. Obviously the farmer had a nest of kestrels which, although worthy of a visit by a licensed ringer, were a little far out for Philip's hectic schedule.

Then, one evening in October, a kestrel was brought in to us from Steeple Claydon. It was very ill and smelt strongly of diesel oil, though there was none marking its rather boldly striped plumage. Was it a kestrel? Or could it be . . .? No, impossible. But yes, it had to be a merlin. Could the farmer have been right after all? A phone call to Philip brought him, ladders flying, to the next door and then in to us. It was a merlin, but Philip thought it had been sprayed with an insecticide which can be carried in a diesel oil solution. He suggested we all wash our hands thoroughly after handling the bird. Contrary to popular belief, there are no antidotes to most poisons, even if we could have identified the toxin in the first place. There was nothing we could for the once proud little bird. We could only give it warmth and quiet, and hope for the best.

Needless to say, it was dead by the morning, another victim of Europe's agricultural policy of spraying everything in order to grow more than we need. Philip called to collect the corpse which would go, along with any other of our failures, into the national collection at the British Museum. A rare bird like a merlin could have been sold for a high price on the taxidermy market and often we have been approached to sell such bodies. However, right from the outset I have taken a stand against the hobby of stuffed birds. Not only does it seem ghoulish but I feel there's a risk that in the search for a good specimen rare birds may be allowed to die or may even be put to sleep – and I know there are still those who will shoot specimens for their glass cases.

On the other hand the collection of skeletons, skins and bodies at the British Museum are kept there for the nation and for bona fide study; and many well-known bird books have been illustrated with drawings based on the specimens in the Museum's archives. Certainly we have always found the skeleton collection most useful when investigating some of the strange intricacies of a bird's frame. One particular instance, shortly after the merlin episode, illustrates just how crucial are the Museum's facilities. We had taken in at the hospital a tawny owl which had flown through the cab window of a train. One eye was so severely damaged that it would have to be removed, but neither the vet nor I had encountered this problem before: an owl's eyes are different even from those of other birds and totally different from those of dogs and cats, as Philip Burton explains much better than I could in *Owls of the World*: '. . . in all birds the eyeball is protected by a ring of small bony plates (scleral-ossicles) which in owls form a long bony tube.' A trip to the Museum's archives gave me perfectly prepared examples of this specification and also the strange sensation of seeing some of our donations to the collection rubbing shoulders with those given by Charles Darwin over a hundred years before.

With the information I gleaned Richard Hill, the vet, was able to execute a perfect operation to remove the eye, being completely prepared for the strange bony structures he was to encounter.

This was just one of the many new and innovative procedures we had to introduce to cope with the vastly varied selection of casualties which were arriving. Luckily, with the influx of casualties there came a fairly regular flow of donations for their support.

Sue had been talking about the situation to two of our neighbours, Philip Dunn and Roy Collins, who turned out to be a barrister and accountant respectively. Together, we all thought it would be in the best interest of all concerned if we formed a registered charity whereby a Board of Trustees oversaw any funds and submitted accounts annually to the Charity Commissioners.

Philip prepared all the necessary documentation including that mass of legal jargon, the Trust Deed, which sets out the structure and and aims and objects of a registered charity. His preparation must have been immaculate for after a very short time the Wildlife Hospital Trust officially received its charter on 1st February 1983, almost five years after Sue and I had first started seriously taking in casualties. Now we could go out and attract donations for the hospital, completely divorcing our own financial situation from that of the animals and birds. Or so we thought, until the first venture of the new Trust needed support from our own meagre resources.

Many of the larger conservation charities thrive on a continuing membership and regular publication of good wholesome literature. When an immature kittiwake, which defied identification for two days, was brought in by a lady from the other side of Aylesbury, we had our first member. Our magazine took a little longer. True, I had the photographs and could write the articles, but we had to attract advertising to finance it and nobble a printer to produce it. We had met a graphic designer, Roger Laishley, over an injured woodcock, in deep snow during the winter. Roger and his wife Marilyn agreed to do the artwork, and, with our friend Ian Mackay offering to do any drawings, we could soon produce our first publication. The only problem was what we would call it. Radio One came up with the answer as 'Bright Eyes', that haunting Mike Batt tune from *Watership Down*, was played just at the right moment to catch our imagination.

Bright Eyes, the magazine, was almost ready to run off the presses, but the advertising income was still £200 short of the production estimate. That's where we came back in. By increasing our own overdraft, we could ensure that the Trust at least started without any debts and the magazine was ready.

It was not long before the television companies began to hear of our genuine involvement with wildlife and to realise that we really did treat and look after wild animals and birds – wonderful television material which they could not resist. Soon the cameras were rolling at Pemberton Close and the people of Britain were seeing, perhaps for the first time, that an injured wild bird or animal could be saved. Of course we realised that this stepping up of publicity would mean more cardboard boxes with more casualties but, if they were injured and needed help, we felt confident that we could fit them in.

At first, going before the cameras was fraught with mis-cues and stumbling hesitations, but Sue and I always analysed each transmission to see if we should improve our technique. True, we did bicker sometimes about who should or should not have said what. However it really wasn't too bad, except for the one time when Sue told all the viewers of BBC's 'South East at Six' that we often 'jump around the garden in our nighties' trying to discourage visiting tawny owls.

People looking at our old videos still eye me with suspicion after that!

Things started to look much brighter on the financial front. The hospital was attracting its own income and inflation had made a fairly big hole in our mortgage repayments, so we too were finding life easier. The only thing the animals were now lacking was space. Our small garden was liberally lined with pens and aviaries but we did need an overflow. Fortunately, when we first acquired the house we bought the piece of land to the side of the property which for all those years had been just an unusable expanse of grass to mow and a place for passers-by to dump their litter. We had planning permission to fence it in, giving us enough room for the time being to cope with more casualties, particularly Bambi, the young fallow deer, who was back on her feet and walking. She, for one, would grow into a very large animal, needing a lot of space and a lot of lawn to eat and trample.

With only one deer we could have coped with the lack of space, but what if another came along? We could have problems and, as my principle was never to turn an animal away, we really did have to think of the future and make contingency plans to move to a more spacious area. Only a short while ago I had wanted, desperately, to up-root and flee to some remote corner of England where we could meet only animals and no people. However, the people around Aylesbury had restored my faith in the human race. Quite unlike the runners in the rat-race of the business world, the people who now knocked on our front door were the kind, caring people who had taken the trouble to stop and pick up an injured bird or animal which needed help. Many have become lasting friends and volunteers at the hospital. How could we possibly leave such people and try to start again elsewhere? No, we decided, we just had to find somewhere nearby and within our price range.

We heard of a deserted Rothschild hunting lodge in nearby Tring which, on investigation, turned out to be an ideal wildlife area. Set in seventeen acres was the remains of an old building. The doors, windows and floors were non-existent but the grounds would have made a wonderful hospital and release area. Laid out as a miniature replica of one of the five Rothschild mansions around Aylesbury,

Blossom did not look anything like a fox.

there was a waist-high lawned area in front of the house running down to a lake where apparently kingfishers used to nest in the high banks. Badly silted up though it was, it would not have taken a team of volunteers long to turn the lake and surrounding grounds into a wildlife centre. The rest of the site was heavily wooded and, just like the open areas, was badly in need of management. The one Rothschild whim which had not, in all these years, fallen into decay was the row of gigantic specimen trees planted along the lake's edge – ancient Wellingtonias and acacias. The site should be looked after, if only for those trees and the potential wildlife habitat which would otherwise fall to developers.

We discovered who owned the site, an old recluse named Joe Eggleton who lived in another patch of overgrown woodland just up the road. Entering his secret garden through an old iron gate set into a giant hedge, we found his house was in not much better condition than the hunting lodge. The roof was sliding to pieces, the windows were cracked and when Joe emerged from his broken-down back door, billows of wood smoke followed him from the dark interior.

Joe had only a couple of teeth and in clothes he had obviously worn for years, he looked the epitome of Compo in 'The Last of the Summer Wine'. We introduced ourselves and got around to talking about the birds in his garden which were flocking to his side. He knew them all, and their Latin names, and had wonderful stories to tell of the flycatchers, the robins and the wood pigeon, his favourite. He showed us around his personal jungle where, amongst the old wooden buckets and milk carts, there was even a relic of a shepherd's hut on wheels with a tree growing through it.

In every old pot or cranny birds were nesting. They were his life, nothing else seemed to matter to him, except, that is, the ladies. For, although he was old and scruffy, his charm and several little posies of wild flowers won Sue over – so much so that at our first encounter we could not broach the subject of the piece of land down the road. For the moment we simply enjoyed Joe's company and his stories of the birds. Perhaps we could ask him about its future later . . .

But we never did. His attitude to life was so completely carefree that it seemed wrong to upset the balance. He had sorted out his values and let nothing bother him. If only I could have adopted his philosophy.

★

Although I had almost forgotten the traumatic events of five years before, I still had a phobia about, of all things, letters arriving in the post. Every bang of the letterbox turned my stomach, as I rushed to find out who was 'persecuting' me this time. A brown envelope, especially marked O H M S, signalled doom and a letter from the bank would knock me down for hours. Poppy, the Cavalier spaniel, would wait, ears cocked, to attack the post in a demented spring to the door but, even then, I often beat her to it. Something drastic was needed to rid me of the obsession but the horrific consequences of my cure will live with me forever and will ensure that never again will I run my life at the beck and call of a second-class stamp.

Blossom was a very young vixen which had been found mewing beside a female fox killed by a hit and run driver. Whether the mother fox had been carrying her cub or had given birth after the accident we shall never know. All we did know was that this little fox club was a genuine orphan who did not have a chance of survival unless we could manage to hand rear it on a powdered puppy-milk substitute.

She did not look anything like a fox: she was brown, her ears were short and stubby and her blunt snout made her look more like a kitten as she suckled happily on the baby's bottle which Sue used to feed her. Additions of baby cereal and mashed dog food soon had her growing well, although every few hours even through the night, she would wake and cry, demanding food and a cuddle from Sue who was becoming terribly attached to her young charge. An old cuddly toy rabbit made a good mother substitute for Blossom to cuddle up to between feeds.

We had a plan to avoid Blossom's becoming permanently reliant on human company because, after all, our purpose in running a wildlife hospital is to get our patients back to the wild. For the moment, I would leave the handling and feeding of the fox to Sue. In that way Blossom would treat Sue as a mother but, at weaning, I would take the fox to an outside pen and have nothing more to do

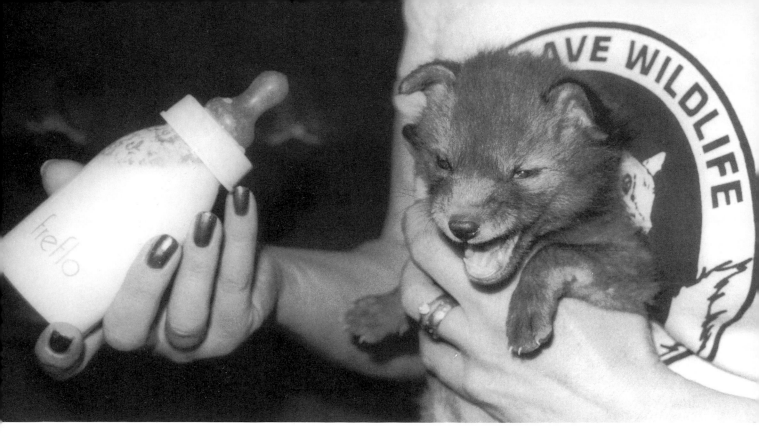

Sue feeding Blossom.

with her other than to give her food and water. In fact, although it may sound cruel, I would have to frighten her, so that when it came to release she would shy away from human beings altogether.

That was the theory but, as we all know, 'The best laid plans of mice and men' have a way of going wrong. Blossom was so charming that no one could help finding her appealing. We had only to walk into the room and she would come bounding over, ears flat, tail sagging, giving little pants of pleasure. We could not resist her.

But she was growing quite large and it became more and more difficult to keep her in her box. The answer seemed to be a play-pen with a false bottom, but with extra bars to stop her squeezing out. It worked well. She had room to run around and amazed us all at her use of a dirt-box from an unbelievably early age. She would still greet us as though we had been away for ever – the wonder of a new puppy a hundred times over.

The small garden was liberally lined with pens and aviaries.

Then the black Friday. I was shaving in the upstairs bathroom when the postman arrived. I couldn't beat Poppy but dropped everything and ran from the bathroom to get the letters. On the second stair down our dark staircase I trod on something and fell from top to bottom, landing on whatever had tripped me. It was Blossom: somehow she had got out of the playpen and was waiting on the stairs. I thought I had broken my arm, but, much worse, Blossom was lying there, blood pouring from her mouth and nose. I had killed her! But no, I found she was still alive. Hugging her to me, I jumped into the car and, arriving at the vet's, ran straight through to the operating theatre. But the vet said it was hopeless: my bulk had crushed the life out of her. Although everybody told me it was an accident, to this day I never take even the slightest notice when the postman arrives, and will never have another wild animal living in the house.

Tring is the 'In' Place

We had made the decision after that horrendous accident not to keep any more wild animals around the house. Some people, however, have no choice when it comes to uninvited lodgers with all manner of mammals, welcome and unwelcome, taking advantage of their own warm, dry nest boxes. Of course, an incursion by rats or mice can explode into a health problem but, all the same, many a country kitchen has willingly offered winter shelter to a family of, not quite so dastardly, wood mice. Bats are now protected by law and, provided there are no chemicals about, may help to keep a home free of many infuriating summer insects. What could be nicer, on a warm evening, than to watch their flittering aerobatics as they go and come to their gently chattering broods hanging in your loft?

Even the heavy-handed squirrel sometimes finds a drainpipe ladder to an attic, but its tenancy is often brought to an abrupt halt to prevent the damage those awesome front teeth may inflict on rafters, wiring and unexpected visitors. If you live within fifteen miles of Tring, in Hertfordshire, be prepared for invasion by Glis glis, a squirrel in miniature. Well known in this area, the Glis glis is not really a squirrel but is in fact a larger cousin of that endearing British mammal, the now exceedingly rare 'common' dormouse. The Glis glis is probably the only animal in the world known by its generic name, but since its non-scientific cognomens are the unflattering 'fat-

Glis glis, a squirrel in miniature.

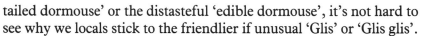

tailed dormouse' or the distasteful 'edible dormouse', it's not hard to see why we locals stick to the friendlier if unusual 'Glis' or 'Glis glis'.

Released around Tring in 1902 by the eccentric Walter Rothschild, these exotic immigrants probably complemented the kangaroos and emus running free on his estate which he toured in an open carriage drawn by zebras. Walter, the kangaroos, emus and zebras have all gone, but the adaptable Glis glis is still with us. They moved into the surrounding countryside, playing havoc with the Forestry Commission, whose hands were fortunately tied by the Wildlife and Countryside Act, the local householders, whose lofts provided wonderful hibernation sites, and the electricity board, whose substations were short-circuited every winter by the nesting animals.

Their status of 'fair game' for local pest controllers is still debatable, but there is no denying that, pretty as they are, they have the gnawing potential of a squirrel and, being much bolder, will often leave their attic nests to cause damage in the rest of the house. We often take in casualties which have been trapped or, as is usually the case, youngsters which have been caught by the family cat.

Being the only wildlife facility in this part of England we must have seemed the obvious people for the BBC's Natural History Unit to contact when they wanted to film, probably for the first time, the invasion of roof-dwelling dormice. Wild Glis glis do not make appointments and, although I know of lofts regularly visited by dozens of animals, we realised that to save days of wasted camera work and possibly disturbing resident dormice, it would be wiser to create our own habitat in the attic of a small white cottage in Tring. Where else?

Lining the whole roof area with polythene would enable us to keep any Glis glis within bounds, as they are capable of phenomenal bursts of speed and can run up walls to escape capture. We had two Glis glis fully recovered and ready to be released into a series of barns but *not* into the surrounding five hundred acres of pastureland, a Glis glis no-go area. We had to take these precautions as it is against the law to release non-indigenous mammals into the *countryside*. (That it is perfectly acceptable to release foreign birds, like pheasants and little owls, but not mammals just shows the anomalies of our wildlife

Tiddler, the Glis glis.

lesiglation.) Our two Glis would make perfect television stars before they were taken to the farm.

The programme was to be fronted by Matthew Woods, a young, keen naturalist from Bristol, whose sole remuneration seemed to be an hourly Mars bar. Nobody had ever filmed Glis in an attic before but our two mega-stars performed handsomely – eating their apples on cue, acrobating under the rafters and, when I eventually caught them, mouthing into the microphone the most horrendous Glis glis obscenities, which sound just like an old motor car refusing to start on a frosty morning. It made superb film, at last capturing this charming little animal for all the country to see.

As with all our casualties which are fit enough, our Glis glis are given a chance of freedom, if only in those voluminous barns, but we have had to keep one particular animal, as he could never survive even a closeted environment. His name is Tiddler, and he was caught by a cat when he was very small. His front legs were paralysed, the nerves having been damaged by his feline assailant, but he took quickly to the bottle and mashed apple and soon showed signs of recovery. Everything was progressing well but as the 'pins and needles' in his left leg indicated life returning, he promptly ate his own foot, leaving just a couple of bone ends exposed. Russell duly tidied it up under anaesthetic, but then Tiddler decided to eat the other foot. This usually spells disaster for, when a mammal has lost more than one limb, it is quite incapable of walking, and has to be put down. But not Tiddler. He was going to prove us wrong and now, with only two and a half legs, he is as mobile as a complete animal. Not only does he walk well on his hind legs, but he runs, climbs and even does acrobatics just like his cousins. He now lives a full life in a large cage with all manner of logs and branches to climb on and gnaw and has a constant throughput of visiting Glis, en route to the farm, to keep him company.

Being strictly nocturnal, he is seen by few people but those who do manage to catch a fleeting glimpse immediately fall for his huge eyes and cuddly appearance.

Our first ever wild snake casualty, however, was not so popular. Sue took the call from Aylesbury prison where a group of prison officers were being kept at bay by an adder, Britain's only indigenous venomous snake. Would I go and rescue them?

A little flap opened in the enormous, intimidating prison door and an eye asked me my business. A great bolt creaked, keys jangled and locks clanged (just like in all those television movies). A small door opened in the big door and I stepped inside only to be confronted by an even huger and more intimidating iron gate with a whole array of gleaming brass locks. Finally I was in the prison proper where there was the ring of warders surrounding a seven foot long net which presumably held the serpent.

Snakes do not worry me, although I do hold them in great respect and will never handle one until I am absolutely sure of its pedigree. Britain has a very small quota of naturally wild snakes, making the three species and the snake look-alike, the slow worm, easily identifiable. The trouble is that with the ever-increasing pet trade in exotic species, there are more and more strange reptiles escaping or being dumped in our countryside. I have come across two harmless Indian pythons, a garter snake and a ferocious Bosc monitor, all of which I

could recognise as non-venomous species, but when it comes to obscure species like mambas and tropical vipers which can kill in an instant, I never take any chances and have imported snake-catching equipment from America, just in case.

Going boldly where none of the prison warders would go, I peered into the depths of the net and, seeing the golden collar which is so typical of the grass snake, plunged my arm in and deftly held the serpent aloft, announcing with relief, 'It's only a grass snake!' Of course, they all then admitted, to a man, that they had known this all the time, and one by one they sidled off to their duties.

The snake was, as all snakes are, a masterpiece of design and elegance, its golden collar contrasting with its dark green back and chequered tummy. It had suffered no injury during its imprisonment but I just had to photograph it before releasing it in a more suitable habitat.

Back at home in my study I set up an aquarium with old logs and leaves to simulate a woodland floor. The grass snake was soon sliding in and out of the nooks and crannies but when I left it, only for a

The snake was a masterpiece of design.

minute or two to collect a casualty at the door, it performed the typical snake-escaping trick and disappeared. My study is, at best, a mass of books, papers, camera equipment and old files but, even after pulling the lot out, I could find no trace of the elusive reptile. To make matters worse, that evening we had arranged a meeting of some of our fund-raising team to organise a stall at the Tring carnival celebrations. Some of the team would not have ventured into the house if there had been a snake in a closed aquarium, let alone sliding on the loose, heavens knew where.

With discretion we did not let the meeting into our little secret and the snake, fortunately, did not make an appearance. In fact, there was still no sign of it the following morning when Sue and I had to go out. On our return, Sue opened the door to find the snake lying on the doormat to greet her. In her surprise and an attempt not to tread on it, she came tumbling out into the drive. We caught the snake and wasted no time before releasing it by a local woodland stream where it could bother no one.

During that particular year we received no end of snake calls. They were all adders which turned out to be grass snakes or slow worms but, in all but one incident, the good news was that people were no longer killing snakes on sight. Perhaps the conservation message that snakes will avoid human contact while taking many garden pests was at last getting through.

I am always advocating that you must first identify your snake but the hissing horror which was haunting a family on Bedgrove housing estate, across town to us, was well hidden from view in a clump of herbaceous border. I arrived nonchalantly and, yes, it certainly sounded like a snake hiding in the flower beds, but which species was it? I don't know if there is anybody who can identify a snake by its hiss but I was not going to take any chances. Brandishing a six foot bean pole, I carefully approached the sound. As I felt with my bean pole the hissing rose in a crescendo then, as I parted the foliage the beast identified itself – a swarm of bees. I didn't see Sue for dust as she fled up the garden, through the French windows and house, back to the car parked out front. I beat a more dignified retreat and then tried to explain the benefits of having bees to the houseowner who was understandably unconvinced after Sue's headlong dash to safety. I will face any snake or British wild animal, but when it comes to bees I prefer to leave it to the experts, the masochistic apiarists, who actually seem to enjoy 'mixing it' with all those stingers.

Sue's dash was the result of an innate terror of any *hymenoptera*, bees, wasps or the much-maligned very docile hornet. The psychologists probably have some name to describe the phobia which is completely uncontrollable. I have a phobia about tax inspectors, but poor Charlie Norris was an ophidiaphobiac, with an inbuilt fear of snakes which, in an RSPCA inspector, can be very embarrassing. Anyhow, the only time Charlie did arrive, with the inevitable grass snake, I had to go out and unload the cardboard box from his van, whereas I had often stood back and marvelled at the way Charlie faced the largest most ferocious dogs or irascible horses and bulls without blinking an eye.

Of course, there is always the fear of mis-identification and the general public are notorious at getting species wrong. But not only where snakes are concerned. We have had countless kingfishers that were really starlings, sparrows that were dunnocks; sparrow-hawks are always kestrels (except the one that was a swift) and seagulls are very often itinerant dovecote pigeons; storks or cranes are always herons because you don't find the former in this country. However, I remember the story told me by the late John Hughes, who was a champion of wildlife care. He had received a call to a stork in a lady's garden and duly went out to round up a heron only to be confronted, on his arrival, by the most aggressive and largest of all storks, a Marabou, which had never been recorded north of its African homeland. Nobody ever came forward to claim it and, when we went to visit John, there it was lording it over the swans and geese in the waterfowl pen. Since then we never dismiss fanciful identifications until we see the animal. Mind you, this Christmas we turned out at two o'clock in the morning to 'a funny green bird' in trouble on an Aylesbury driveway only to find a town pigeon looking none too well. I don't know who had indulged in too much Christmas cheer, the caller or the pigeon. Still, Andy and I didn't mind going out to rescue the bird at that unearthly hour of the morning: the pigeon needed treatment and the lady who called could not bring it herself as she was in her nightie.

You would think, reading this chapter, that all the aggressive creatures come from abroad, but this is far from the case. There is one bird which is frequently cardboard-boxed into the hospital, as it can be positively lethal. That bird is the great crested grebe, which is now found at many of Britain's open reservoirs and lakes after a recovery from near extinction earlier this century. The great crested grebe bears no resemblance whatsoever to its docile smaller cousin, the little grebe, which we had come to know so well the previous winter. On one occasion eleven cardboard boxes were delivered at one time, each holding a great crested grebe trying to dismantle its container and permanently maim its rescuer. They had all been rounded up from a flooded sand quarry which carried a surface-layer of diesel oil leaked from a nearby tank. Many of the birds were

Each box held a great crested grebe.

smothered in the oil and one had even smashed its beak to pieces in its frenzy to escape from its box.

Washing oiled birds with the now recognised Newcastle system is a two-person job, though I had the feeling that each of these squawking, stabbing grebes was going to be more than a match even for two people. But before we could even contemplate the cleaning we had to try to save the birds' damaged digestive systems, both with medication and by getting them to eat as often as possible. Happily, all but the bird with the broken beak had soon turned their stabbing attention from us to the dishes of whitebait we offered, so we could then safely leave them unmolested and unwashed for at least three days.

At ninety pence per pound whitebait was on a par with other expensive foodstuffs, like mealworms at sixty pence an ounce and monkey nuts at fourteen pounds a bag, which we had to buy in. Fundraising was becoming, after the actual care of the patients, the second most important of the Trust's activities. The meeting on the 'night of the snake' had been to arrange an appearance at the Tring carnival. By then we had our own tent, which kept most of the rain off and a varied selection of bric-à-brac, books, antiques, plants and boxes of double-sided sticky pads generously donated by DRG Kwikseal and which brought in a lot of money. All along I had tried to emphasise the 'fun' in fundraising and each weekend saw a day or two of enjoyable busking.

On the eve of the carnival we received a mysterious phone call asking if we were still looking for a new site for the hospital and if Sue and I would be at Tring the following day. Yes, on both counts, especially the latter for, in spite of all the volunteer help we received, we still had to attend each and every function where the Trust was represented. But we had no idea who the caller was or why he wanted to know. Could it be that ethereal benefactor who, we promised ourselves, would turn up out of the blue some day? We would have to wait until the next day to find out.

Yet somehow in all the time we knew John Fyson we were never really sure what the outcome of our discussions might be. A man of boundless energy, in spite of his age of over eighty, John had since the war virtually built his manor house at Chalfont St Giles with his own hands. He seemed to have done everything in his time and had made a success of it, including the house in Chalfont which he let off in flats to families who had no roof over their heads.

His interest in us was that there were a few acres of land next to the manor which had been used as a field kitchen during the war but more recently as a motor repair centre. If we could obtain planning permission and could repair the buildings, we could site our hospital there and possibly have the use of more land at the back of the main house.

However, after some stormy Council meetings, we were unable to get the necessary planning permission. It looked as though our ship hadn't come in and we would just have to increase our fundraising profile. Our next venture was to be a celebrity football match between the TV Entertainers XI and Aylesbury United Football Club. We were determined to make it work and for a full three weeks before the big day every night (and it rained every night) saw us out knocking on doors selling tickets. To ensure at least a modicum of success and to attract wives and families to a football match we also arranged for a fête to take place within the grounds followed by a disco in the evening, and were grateful to Aylesbury United Football Club for allowing us the use of their ground for both the fête and the match.

On the Sunday morning of the match the rain was still coming down and once again we all got soaked but at least we were happy in the knowledge that, even if nobody turned up, we had already collected £1000 by door-knocking. However, at lunchtime, right on cue, the sun came through and the procession of cars told us we were not going to flop.

All our volunteers had designated jobs. Jenny Babb, our membership secretary, was to receive any money collected on the gate or at the stalls. She appeared early accompanied by a tall young man whom, we all assumed, was a friend. We thought nothing more of it. Then he appeared in the public address booth helping to play the records. Next thing he was on the field in shorts and football strip. After the match the players were ferried back to the hospital to see

Wildlife hospital turned down: 'We will appeal'

A WILDLIFE hospital would be excellent Blue Peter material — but not in Chalfont St Giles.

That was the verdict of Chiltern District Council planning committee on Thursday of last week when members thought it was a good idea to have somewhere to care for sick animals, but not in the green belt.

The councillors' main opposition to Les Stocker's proposals was that he also wanted to convert a storage building into a single-storey dwelling.

They refused the application but afterwards Mr Stocker, who, with his wife Sue, runs the Wildlife Hospital Trust from their Aylesbury home, said he would appeal against the decision.

Councillor Donald Phillips said: "This is a very sensitive spot. The site is a repository for random dumping and we would like it to be cleared up.

"But development is justified only if the community is going to be benefited. The primary objective is to get a housing unit in the green belt and this is not appropriate. I fear we may end up with some creeping utilisation of this area."

Councillor Phillips thought that Mr Stocker's claim that only five vehicles a day would visit the site was challengeable.

He said that as something like 2,000 animals a year had been looked after by the Stockers it "makes one wonder if five is a realistic forecast"

Councillor Phillips added: "I am opposed to the position, not the animal sanctuary. I really believe this is not the right spot."

Councillor John Breadmore said: "This is excellent Blue Peter material with visits from parties of schoolchildren. But not in the green belt."

He queried why Mr Stocker, whose present hospital operates in a garden measuring 12 metres by 18 metres, needed to move on to a site of about an acre.

"Are they to carry out research?" he asked and also voiced his concern for wildlife, such as badgers, who already used the site.

Mike Hartley, chief planning officer, did not make any recommendation but admitted he considered that a reasonable case exists for granting planning permission.

Members decided by six votes to five that they were "not minded" to giving approval and then turned down the plan.

Outside the council chamber, Mr Stocker said: "We need a bigger area because there is just not enough room in our garden. I would like to point out we don't research any animals. 'Research' is a nasty, nasty word.

"We knew about the badger sets. You are not allowed by law to disturb them and we have no intention of disturbing them.

"One of the councillors called it an animal sanctuary. It is a hospital not a sanctuary."

Mrs Stocker said only one councillor accepted an open invitation to visit their home to see what work is done, but she was happy with the attitude of the council officials who she described as being civil and helpful.

the work we were doing and, lo and behold, there he was in one of the cars. Who was he? Jenny had assumed he was a volunteer whom I had conscripted into her service. Nobody seemed to know who he was. It was about time I asked him, but he seemed to have disappeared into thin air.

Perhaps we had seen the last of our mystery helper but, no, when the local papers came out a week later there he was grinning up at us

IF FOOTBALL'S your cup of tea why not pitch the family together and take them to Aylesbury United FC on Sunday.

For there wil be a match with a difference as a star-studded cast aim to knock spots off Aylesbury United and raise funds for the local Wildlife Hospital.

Some of the celebrities expected to dribble their skills will be former Monkees singer Davy Jones, Blue Peter star Peter Duncan and Gary Tibbs of Adam and the Ants fame.

Other celebrities forming the TV Entertainers XI team will include Christopher Quinton of Coronation Street, Simon Groom, Roy Holder and there will be guest appearances by footballer Alan Hudson and some of his Chelsea team-mates. Gates open at 2pm and the match kicks off at 3pm.

Lizzie had the daunting task of bathing him.

from the photographs! I've just re-read all the newspaper cuttings of the event: Aylesbury United won by six goals to three, over fifteen hundred people attended and the Trust raised nearly three thousand pounds. And he is still there grinning back at me. Who was he?

Mysteries were regularly cropping up at the Trust. I mean, nobody really understands the secret of birds and toad migration, or why a hedgehog self-lathers or a bird puts ants under its feathers, yet my next mystery had to be man-made. In Tring, once again, I received a report of a badger in a pit. Immediately the vision of badger-baiting in a pit spring to mind so, wasting no time, I headed for the site, which was actually outside the town at the edge of a field on a steep bank above the Cholesbury road. Ready for anything and with badger-catching equipment at the ready, we searched the area, and nearly fell into the pit. Not the sort of pit I had expected, but a small hole in the ground, only 18 inches across, with a bell-shaped pit underneath it, at least twenty feet in diameter and twenty feet deep. In our torch light, at the bottom of the pit, we could see the badger frantically trying to dig its way out. There was no way I could possibly get down to it without a ladder and dropping a rope would have been no use. So, it was back to Aylesbury to fetch the ladder. My first rescue attempt was foiled because I could not get through the hole at the top. We had not brought any tools for digging and had the long laborious task of chipping away at the hole with penknives and the badger stick. Eventually I could get through and, as I descended, grasper in hand, the stench hit me and thoughts of methane and coal gas crossed my mind. However, the badger was still alive: things couldn't be too bad. Literally hundreds of animals must have died in that pit. In fact, two dead foxes looked to have been half eaten, probably by the badger. I dared not risk standing on the floor in case I sank into mud, so I stood on the bottom rung and chased the badger with the loop of the grasper. Once I had caught him, there was no way I could get us both together through the hole, so I held him dangling below me on the grasper as I climbed out and pulled him after me. He stank of the muck and decay from the bottom of the pit.

With him safely in a basket, we covered the pit with planks of wood and let the farmer know of the potential death trap hidden

He waddled off through the corn.

amongst his corn. Why the pit was there and what purpose it served had us all flummoxed. Perhaps some local historian could shed some light on its purpose.

As for the badger, he had to be bathed. A task not to be taken lightly. I could not possibly contemplate such a dangerous task by myself. The badger would have to be anaesthetised. A job for the vet whose staff were less than pleased by the awful smell I was taking into their nice clean surgery. One of the nurses, Lizzie, had the daunting task of bathing him, while I held him, but once the badger was

shampooed and dried, he looked just like a cuddly teddy bear. That was until he came round from the anaesthetic and expressed his feelings at being kept in a small cage.

He seemed no worse for his ordeal and toilet so the following night we took him back to the same field at Tring and watch him waddle off through the corn back to his sett. Oh, the stories he could tell.

★

Tring is seven miles from Aylesbury and over the years we have become more and more familiar with people of this affable town nestling in a crook of the Chiltern Hills. Quite unlike many other small towns, Tring's industry has, in the main, been there for years so the town is little scarred by those faceless industrial estates which usually gobble up any open space available. The High Street, however, used to be impassable but now that the town has its own by-pass, the High Street is no longer a tarmac death trap for hundreds of toads which every spring make their laborious trek from the surrounding gardens and countryside, to the ancestral breeding ponds tucked cosily behind the local houses.

Some do still get squashed, but now, each year, help is at hand from a team of toad lifters initiated by our Trust. Our nextdoor neighbour, Nigel Brock, has become so involved with local amphibian crises that he jumped forward as organiser of the toad lifts, much to the consternation of his wife, Sharon, who light-heartedly complains that each night he takes books on toads to bed and sits up until all hours reading them.

Many of the crossing points which I discovered years ago out in the country are now devoid of toads. Perhaps it was the increased use of insecticides on farmland which killed them off or because many of the watercourses are poisoned with the run-off from the land. We still see a few searching for the stream which used to run along the edge of Aylesbury but that has now been imprisoned in a pipe, denying the amorous amphibians their conjugal rights. We used to try to save the occasional struggling toad but often, as we stopped the car to jump out to the rescue, a following car would overtake and, 'splat', there was one more toad less. Walking this stretch of unlit country lane resulted in our saving one or two toads from the

constant traffic but the danger to the rescue team, unfortunately, was far too great. Then Nigel found out about the crossing-point in the centre of Tring. Since the by-pass had been in service and the town traffic decimated, far more toads were appearing; with proper organisation it seemed likely that a safety-conscious rescue network could be built up.

The Trust purchased fluorescent safety jackets and white buckets for carrying the toads. Nigel managed to salvage some orange warning beacons, while the Fauna and Flora Preservation Society provided a pair of road signs to make drivers aware of the hazard. A couple of referee's whistles would warn of any approaching traffic and with volunteers clamouring to go out on windy, wet March evenings, we were ready to go, at the first sign of a toad on its way to its breeding pond.

Any motorist passing through Tring on one of those dark, dank evenings would be mystified by the apparitions appearing before him. Firstly, a peculiar road sign accompanied by a flashing beacon and a shrill whistle while, beyond that, groups of dumpy figures with yellow jackets, carrying torches and white buckets, were bending up and down in the road. 'Must be a Round Table stunt or something? Better slow down just in case. Crikey, I nearly ran over a toad.'

Our team's presence did not always have this effect on motorists but it certainly helped the toads. There was a friendly rivalry to see who could save the most toads which, at the end of the evening, could run into hundreds. We made startling discoveries about the toads' migration. Many of them fell into roadside drains and swam around until exhausted. Two men from the team were then regularly despatched, armed with a lever and kiddies' fishing net to scour the drains, rescuing toads by the dozen and even one newt. An old factory complex was in the toads' direct path to their pond and many were found floundering, lost in its maze of walls and pathways. Whoever patrolled this complex always had the highest returns, winning the accolades of the evening.

At first, some of the women were a little hesitant to pick up the toads but, after they had made the acquaintance of a big, fat, matriarchal old female or a rampant, croaking 'I'll make love to

Groups of dumpy figures with luminous jackets.

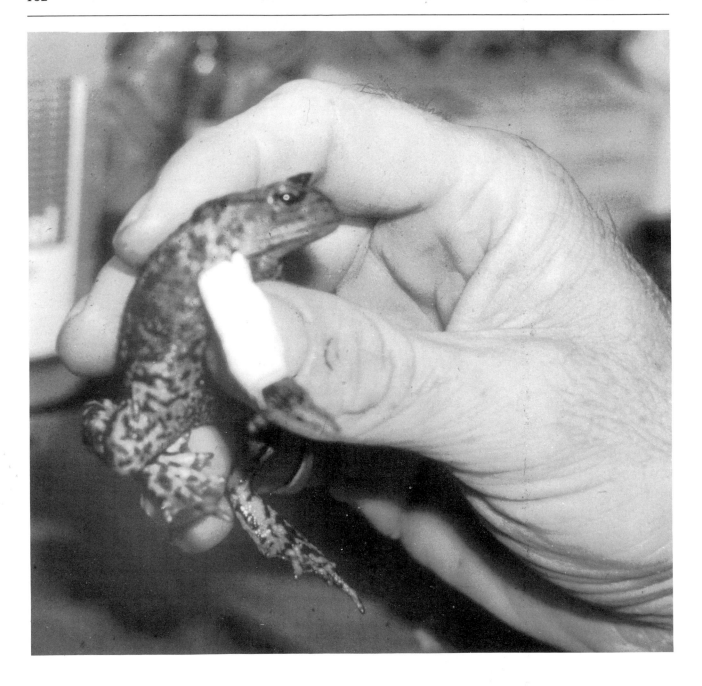

anything' smaller male, they were soon vying for the prolific factory site and even delving into drains. Of course, on the roads themselves were the pathetic little bodies of those which had not made it across. My grisly, but sometimes rewarding task when I found one alive, was to count these casualties for the nationwide survey carried out each year by Tom Langton of the FFPS. In fact, all the toads in the buckets were counted: the big single toads were invariably female; the males all croaked when touched, a warning device to prevent two of them fruitlessly trying to mate with each other; and those pairs in amplexus and inseparable were a female being clasped by an amorous male.

The treatment of those injured on the road is still very much in its infancy. However, John Cooper has written many papers on his veterinary work with the lower vertebrates and, applying some of his techniques and plenty of improvisation, we are managing to suture skin wounds and mend fractures. When we first started treating hedgehogs there was very little known about them, but now they are sent to St Tiggywinkles from all over the country. We are now offering the same facilities for toads and, although we may lose some, I know that eventually we shall master the techniques and be able to show others our experiences and methods, so saving even more amphibians who otherwise would have been lost to the motor car.

Finally, on toads, let me recommend a good night out. Get yourself a torch and a bucket, wait for a rainy evening in late March, then go out and help a few toads across the road in the direction they are heading. Funnily enough, it's great fun and everybody enjoys doing something to help wildlife, especially if the coffee at the end of the evening is laced with a dash of brandy. One thing, though, don't forget your 'Green Cross Toad'.

Successfully mending toad fractures.

Weathering a Crisis

Britain's erratic weather has a far more devastating effect on its wildlife than anything else nature can throw at it. At the Hospital the birds in particular can shrug off ice and snow, that is as long as I, too, brave the elements to keep their water bowls from freezing. However, leave them exposed for only an hour in pouring rain and you can count the bedraggled corpses. I only hope that a similar dripping fate does not await our gallant team of volunteers who seem to get soaked through every time I ask them to do something!

Our task this time was to round up four swans and various ducks which had been embroiled in a feather-choking oil spill on Aylesbury's canal basin. Of course, it rained as we caught them and then we got even wetter when washing them to remove the oil, followed by another dowsing as we released them on a rain-driven reservoir some time later. Then they flew back to their oil-bath, causing us to go through the whole dripping procedure all over again.

Barely had the team dried out then I had them all on the streets again, to sell raffle tickets for our second major fundraising venture.

The unwilling perpetrators of the oil spill had been a demolition company obliterating the old factory of Hazell, Watson and Viney, a dark satanic print mill which had dominated the Tring Road out of Aylesbury for over a hundred years. Soaring above the demolition site stood one of Aylesbury's landmarks, Hazell's Chimney, 93 feet of old, black, lifeless bricks that would soon have to join the other piles of rubble at its feet.

You are probably asking yourself, 'What's an old chimney got to do with wildlife?' I must admit that at first I saw no connection between the doomed chimney and our saving those swans. Not so Jez Holder, the tall, suave salesman amongst our volunteers. One morning, while driving past the moonscape that was now Hazell's, he looked up at the chimney, exposed and erect and shouted to himself, 'Why not raffle off the chance to press the button to blow up Hazell's chimney?' He didn't go to work that day. Instead, he came round to the Hospital and, with Sue, sold the site owners and demolition men their retribution by allowing our raffle winner to blow it up.

Out came the raffle tickets, out came the volunteers and down came the rain. But the fun stayed in the fundraising. The people of Aylesbury loved the idea and rather than the 'Oh, no, not another door-to-door collection,' we had whole families laughing, really wanting to win, as they bought their tickets. We were all worn out, with permanently wrinkled fingers by the day of the demolition, but we had raised £2,500 for the birds and animals and we had a winner, Mrs Sue Sandall, who had never won anything in her life before.

Thank goodness it stopped raining for the great day and, just before eleven o'clock, into the site, sipping champagne, floated Sue Sandall in a gleaming white Rolls Royce driven by Mr Eddie Ayres, another of our volunteer team, who had provided his wonderful car to make sure that Sue Sandall's day started with a bang.

At exactly eleven o'clock, Sue Sandall, properly attired in her own peterman's hard hat, knelt, finger poised, above the button. The police stopped all the traffic on the nearby roads, the large crowd craned their heads to see, all the cameras were cocked and ready to go. The siren blasted and echoed eerily across the neighbouring cemetery as the crowd hushed. 'There will be a delay after the explosion,' we were told. Sue waited for the all clear then, with a deafening 'Boom!' a great cloud of smoke and dust gushed from the base of the chimney; the cameras clicked and the motor winders whirred; we all waited in absolute silence for the final demise of the chimney. We knew there was to be a delay. But nothing happened; it didn't even totter. The smoke and dust cleared, revealing a gaping hole at the bottom of the chimney. Still no movement. 'There is no way it won't come down in one,' the engineer had said. Five, then ten minutes passed. Then a solitary reluctant figure was spotted sidling up to the wounded chimney. 'There's one brick holding it up,' came the walkie-talkie message. 'We'll have to set another charge.' Another man made the precarious trip to the base of the glowering chimney to set more charges. The traffic rolled and the crowd breathed again while I joined both the Sues in some of that champagne.

Eventually, after an hour of heart-stopping work by the engineers, they were ready to go again. The traffic stopped, the siren sounded, the crowd was silent; then there was a second 'Boom', and another wait. At last, very slowly and sadly, the once proud chimney started to sink. Its great back broken, it folded in the middle and died with a crunch amongst the other anonymous rubble. A great sad cheer went up and our second major fundraising venture was successfully over. Then it started raining again.

★

All through the early months of the year we are presented with casualties, not only of the rain but often of the wind. Especially if there is a north-easterly gale blowing, we end up with pelagic (ocean going) birds that would be out of place one hundred yards inland let alone in Aylesbury, right in the centre of England. We have had a little auk which crash-landed fifty yards from the Hospital; Godzilla, the black-throated diver and an arctic skua hopelessly miles off course. However, when the telephone jangled me out of bed at one o'clock in the morning, though I knew it would be the police, I assumed there must be an owl or deer in trouble – not a puffin, a bird I had always been enchanted by but had never seen. Yet it was true: a motorway patrol from High Wycombe police station had come across a puffin waddling along the M40 towards Oxford. As usual, we did not know how he got there or where he was going, but we could be

NOW you have the chance to fulfil all your fantasies in one go — ride in a white Rolls Royce, blow up a chimney, and help save wildlife.

That is what is promised for the winner of a raffle being held in aid of Aylesbury's Wildlife Hospital Trust.

But the good news follows some bad. A cygnet from the family of swans, whose story we reported in the Bucks Herald last week, has died from ingesting oil.

Workmen from the Hazells, Watson and Viney site the oil leaked from were so worried about the swans they made a donation to the hospital, and promised to do anything they could.

So when one of the hospital committee members, Mr. Steve Holder, drove past the chimney, and thought of blowing it up as a raffle prize, the demolition company were pleased to help.

The company, W. F. Button and Son Ltd., also organised some of the legal arrangements.

And Mr. Eddie Ayres, who in the 70s made the pop record Hari Krishna, and has recently become involved in the trust's work, has offered his white Rolls Royce to transport the lucky winner.

The demolition will take place on March 10, and the raffle will be drawn on March 8 at Aylesbury United Social Club.

sure he was hungry. So, while they arranged to bring him over, I made an expedition into one of the freezers to chip away for some whitebait.

They had twenty miles to come across country, time enough for me to get dressed, have another cup of tea and check on my resident patients in the garage which had become our intensive care unit. Percy, the pigeon with two broken legs, fluttered in his cradle and knocked his food and water over; another sparrow had escaped his cage and dive-bombed the window at the end of the garage while a hedgehog had managed to crawl under the tray in the incubator which the British Petroleum Company had just bought for us. I should have stayed in bed. Anyway, listening for our extraordinary door buzzer with one ear, I sorted them all out and went back to another cup of tea while I waited. Three quarters of an hour had already gone by; they should be arriving fairly soon. I wondered if they would have their blue light flashing – that would get the neighbours talking.

No sign of them. I thought I might as well adjourn to the study and do my monthly accounts. It's always a surprise to our treasurer, Roy Collins, when I present him with the figures before the end of the following month. Not bad, I had them finished in an hour. Still no police car. Might as well dive into the pile of correspondence to be dealt with. I wondered what had happened. Sometimes people phone us with a casualty then don't turn up because it has died. I hoped this wasn't the case this time. No, they had probably been waylaid by a road traffic emergency. At least, for once, by the time they appeared I would be as wide awake as they were.

They arrived four cups of tea later, at twenty to six. Not a sleek, powerful motorway patrol car but a typical Aylesbury panda. A police constable and police woman presented themselves at the door. I had beaten them to the buzzer – no point in waking Sue and Colin. A quick peek inside the cardboard box revealed the puffin. Isn't it funny how, when you eventually see a bird, in the flesh so to speak, it always looks so much smaller than you ever imagined – and, in this case, where was the Technicolor beak? The books never tell you that they only add this adornment during the breeding season; we were in

Puff'n'Stuff, the puffin.

the throes of winter. He looked up at me and moved his eyes, a thing I had never known any bird able to do. It gave him a whole new attitude, as though he were thinking about me just like a little old man would. It was eerie. I remember Guy the gorilla at London Zoo and how his eyes would follow you, crying out in disdain and despair. This little puffin could surely not have the same feelings? No, I was crediting him with a similar intelligence: that's one of my failings, anthropomorphism.

A cup of coffee loosened the tongues of the two police visitors. Apparently, patrol cars from other districts do not stray into neighbouring manors. The motorway patrol had delivered 'Puff 'n' Stuff' to Wycombe police station where he had waited for an available panda car to ferry him to Amersham; another wait for a panda car to take him on to Aylesbury, and then the final lap to the Hospital. Nearly five hours to cover twenty miles. It's a wonder he wasn't car sick. There I go again, anthropomorphism.

Mind you, being inland in our polluted environment he would more than likely develop the chronic respiratory complaint, aspergillosis. Caused by the fungus aspergillus, this alone kills more sea birds in captivity than any other case. When we were treating Godzilla, the black-throated diver, Richard Hill, our vet at the time, came up with a human drug, Miconazole, that had some effect on this previously untreatable condition. Puff 'n' Stuff would have to be put onto it immediately but the drawback was going to be that the drug is a gel which has to be given orally and a puffin's beak is a formidable weapon. However, with his paddle feet flapping fruitlessly, I did manage to hold him and get the first dose between those pincer jaws, though it nearly cost me one or two fingers.

From then on I let him live free, padding round the garden, occasionally stopping to survey his surroundings with those great moving eyes. He avidly tucked into the whitebait but never once performed the puffin *pièce de résistance* of capturing seven or eight fish all at one time, crosswise in his bill. To offset the thiamine deficiency of his whitefish diet he also had to have a daily pill of vitamin B complex, another daily wrestling match. He joined the other birds on the lawn: the black-headed gull learning to fly again,

the two recuperating ducks and 'Squire' the lapwing who always seemed to find the invisible worm, much to the consternation of the others who all chased him round trying to pirate his prize.

Gradually more mammals were being brought to us and we found caring for them was a whole different ball game. Many were very young, requiring bottle feeding and toilet stimulation. Quite unlike the young birds, who would just sit there and gape, eat and defecate, the young mammals demanded company and comfort, and most of them had their own cuddly toy to cling to as a surrogate mother.

Biddy was an adorable badger cub. Built like a cuddly toy, she was found crying in a wood near Hemel Hempstead. Since she was far too young to have left the sett of her own accord, we could only assume that her home had been disturbed, probably by badger baiters.

An immediate hit with Sue, Biddy took easily to bottle feeding and soon started to put on weight and gain strength. At that time, early in 1984, not only were we very busy with multifarious animals and birds, but were were also trying to organise our first Open Day. We had no room at the Hospital to show people the work we were doing and, anyway, most of the patients would have gone into instant shock at the mere mention of a crowd. Instead, we had to seek a prestige venue in the town centre: the Civic Centre seemed the ideal place, and what's more it was under cover.

For three whole months I pushed, encouraged and cajoled over a hundred volunteers into preparing stands and exhibits all to be set up on the day in the main hall. I saw the Open Day as a platform to show people the many aspects of the Trust's involvement both with wildlife welfare and with basic conservation while combining it with a secondary purpose: that of fundraising. And the idea was to make it a good day out for all the family.

Bill Oddie and Gordon Beningfield, both great friends of the Trust, added the necessary star quality and soon we had people queuing all the way round the Market Square. There was plenty to see, with forty-two specially constructed stands, most of which would interest anybody even remotely concerned with the environment. The fundraising was deliberately low-key but people flocked to the raffle, the tombola and especially the 'Find the Lucky Spines'

Biddy and Spitfire – two orphans together.

in a giant hedgehog. The whole day was a resounding success, with over five thousand people passing through the turnstile. We raised over £7,000 for the Trust, while the Civic Centre took more money in one day at their little coffee bar than they have ever done before or since.

Looking back, we did make one or two mistakes. We tried to show some of the animals which would not be perturbed by the occasion. The toads and frogs, oblivious to all that was going on around them, showed many people, especially the children, that they were not slimy and horrible, while the harvest mice scampered up and down their corn stalks, fussily busy with their mouse house-keeping. The weasel, in the biggest fish tank we could manage, didn't put in an appearance, preferring to stay nestled in his rotten-log home. It was Biddy who was the problem. I thought that people would like to see a live badger cub and, as Biddy was used to people at the Hospital, I could see no harm in taking her along, if only for a brief appearance. That was my mistake. Biddy took one look and sniff at the bustle and the light and buried herself in my shoulder, whickering her own little cry of fear. A good cuddle soon quietened her down but for the rest of the day she remained safely tucked up with her teddy bear in one of the dressing rooms, under the watchful eye of young Trevor Mayne, who had helped to rear her back at the Hospital.

Never again have we asked an animal like Biddy to appear in public, a lesson easily learnt and acted upon. But the other lesson Biddy taught us is a matter not so easily corrected. We have now learnt to take precautions against a young animal or bird imprinting itself onto human beings, that is adopting one of us as its mother. With Biddy it was too late: she grew up to like humans and to trust them and, with the alarming increase in 'terrier men' digging up badgers for sale to 'baiting rings', I dare not attempt to release her to the wild. True, she does share a pen and dry nest box with Granny, a very old badger with arthritis. Every night now, as I go out and talk to her, I cry a little inside at her imprisonment and tell her that one day soon she will have her very own sett and field and wood, at the new Hospital, where she will be able to run, dig and fluff herself up. I think Biddy more than anything else keeps me pushing ahead to

achieve the new Hospital which is now becoming a reality but at that time was just a pipedream with several thousand po nds towards it.

Previous to that memorable day in April we had always looked outside Aylesbury for our support, but on that day the people of the town showed us that they were right behind us. In fact they wanted more open days. They revelled in the work we were doing in our quiet but busy little world at 1 Pemberton Close. Everything around us was looking so much brighter, spring was with us once more with its new life and, of course, all those gaping-mouthed orphans. Although we were losing the good friends who had lived next door since we first moved in six years ago, the new neighbours and their friends seemed very amiable as they leant over the low wire back fence and marvelled at the birds. They were not due to move in for some months but at weekends we let their workers plug into our electricity so they could get their house ready.

They would not have been able to see Bambi and Fate, the fallow deer which had had to be restricted to the land on the opposite side of the house. We were sometimes full to the gunwales but thought we could always take in more without sinking, though the third fallow deer did create a temporary panic.

Derek Read and I went out on the evening call which we assumed would be for a tiny muntjac deer hit by a car and sitting motionless by the side of a country road at Oakley, a small village not far from Aylesbury. What we found stopped us in our tracks while we figured out how to handle it. A full grown fallow buck, weighing at least 150lbs, was sitting on the grass verge, oblivious to the small group of people standing around him. Oblivious, that was, until he spotted the man with the gun just longing to sport him as a trophy for his freezer. We had no time to contemplate any longer, as the deer stood up, the gun went to the shoulder and both Derek and I rugby-tackled the deer to prevent its escape and shield it from the 'sportsman'. For his pains, Derek received a deer kick to his stomach, protected by the enormous plate buckle of his belt while I was on the receiving end of a pile-driver to the jaw. No doubt I saw stars but I could also see that gun, so I hung on to the buck for all I was worth. A fellow living

opposite produced a rope and when we'd hobbled the deer, Derek and I managed to manhandle him into the back of the car.

The deer was surprisingly quiet for the journey back to Aylesbury which, in retrospect, was probably the result of a concussive injury. My jaw was aching so I knew how he felt. Back at the Hospital we managed somehow to off-load him onto the kitchen floor where, spread-eagled, he did not leave room for anything else. Sue in the meantime had phoned the vet, who, when he arrived, could find nothing physically wrong with the deer and, as we did, assumed it to be suffering from a head injury. He administered a mild sedative to keep the deer manageable while we found it suitable accommodation. We could not possibly keep him in the Hospital but he would need watching for some time and he really needed to be housed where he could be easily released, because a fallow buck is virtually impossible to handle when he is fully recovered. Sally's farm in the hills above Tring seemed ideal and, as we expected, Sally jumped with joy at the thought of having a deer to look after.

Back into the car went the deer (I was sure he was getting heavier by the minute) and we set off for Sally's. She had cleared the end of a barn and we all joined in to build a small enclosed area out of hay bales, to keep the deer under some restraint.

Then we went back to the car to fetch the deer, who had made no attempt to move. Derek held its rump while I picked up the head but, having got him out of the car, we both sank to the ground. Exhaustion had got the better of us; we could not lift him another inch and the barn was a good fifty feet away. Sally had the answer – a wheelbarrow. So this proud fallow buck suffered the indignity of a ride in a wheelbarrow, head hanging over one end and legs sticking out at all angles, but it served the purpose and we soon had him in the barn.

By then it was time to look into my own problems. My jaw was throbbing and I was sure I could feel it creak as I moved it. On the way home, we paid a visit to the Casualty Department at Stoke Mandeville Hospital, just to have it checked out. By this time it was past midnight so I more or less had Casualty to myself. Only then did I realise that I reeked of that musky deer smell which may be

ACTION

Injured small wild mammals

Check the casualty for severe bleeding or fly strike (i.e. eggs or maggots). Place a pressure pad over any haemorrhage. Remove all fly eggs or maggots. Do not bother with fleas, ticks or other ectoparasites.

Bring the casualty into the house. Place in a warm dry cardboard box on a covered hot water bottle.

Offer either a shallow dish or, carefully, a pipette of Lectade (available from vets) or glucose water.

Bathe any wounds with dilute Savlon. Do not apply ointments.

Take the casualty to a sympathetic vet or reputable rescue centre.

irresistible to fallow does but has quite the reverse effect on nurses. I had a hard time explaining away my pungent aroma.

I had lost two fillings but no teeth and needed an x-ray to determine whether there was damage to the jaw itself. The machine for x-raying jaws is like one of those brain-sapping contraptions they used in old Boris Karloff movies and, as it started to revolve around my head, I began to wonder if I would end up as a vegetable. I survived, my brain intact, as was my jaw, and would have to manage on paracetamol for a few days until the bruising subsided.

It took the fallow buck a little longer to recover and for the next three weeks the vet visited him regularly and Sally spent many nights just sitting with him. But after three weeks he seemed to come alive again. The concussion had receded and, as if something had switched him back on, he was on his feet and raring to go. And when a fallow buck wants to go, he goes.

He picked the right moment to take himself off our hands as the weather, which had been temperamental for so long, suddenly changed. The clouds disappeared, the sun came out and shone for weeks on end. It was glorious but typical of British weather – too much of a good thing: the heatwave became a drought, water was rationed and all of a sudden the phone started ringing with reports of suffering hedgehogs. Everywhere, it seemed, there were hedgehogs out and about in the daytime, lying in the sun, dying.

We had our own problems with this prolonged hot spell. Many of our birds and animals are fed on meat and meat products and have the infuriating habit of caching away anything they cannot eat at one sitting. In weather like that any scrap of meat is a magnet for flies and, though we fed the patients at night, it was a laborious task, every morning, to search out any potential trouble spots. We managed to keep on top of the problem, even occasionally breaking the embargo on hosepipes just to keep the garden spotless.

This was just as well for, on probably the hottest day of the year, and just as we were celebrating the moving-in of our nextdoor neighbours, we were pole-axed by a visit from a charming young lady from the Public Health Division of the local Council, informing us that an anonymous complaint had been received about the conditions

St Tiggywinkles and some of the aviaries.

in our garden. Now, we were very proud of the way we had been combating the drought and had no hesitation in allowing her to inspect every corner of the Hospital. She was complimentary and even commented that it was a pity some normal gardens were not kept as clean. She could find no grounds for complaint and thought, as we did, that the complaint might have been a malicious fabrication, but from whom we could not imagine.

While all this was going on, we still had to do something to help all those poor hedgehogs and I am pleased to say that this is where the much-maligned people of the media stepped in to avert a disaster situation. We had already set aside one part of the Hospital as 'St Tiggywinkles', the world's first specialist hedgehog unit, where we would willingly take any hedgehog suffering from the heat, but we needed to broadcast to the people of Britain just how they could and should help their local 'pricklies'. The response was enormous and spontaneous. Within hours, every television channel was ringing the warning bells. Within days, most of the national newspapers had articles on hedgehog First Aid and ways to help the neighbourhood hedgehogs and, of course, other wildlife. I am certain that their prompt action was responsible for preventing a major catastrophe from which hedgehogs might never have recovered.

We received another call from a Health Inspector in response to a further complaint, but, like his colleague, he could find no cause for concern. He did, however, give us a clue as to where the 'dagger thrusts' were coming from. He also told us that a dead mouse found on a driveway had been blamed on us but, as the Health Inspector pointed out, it didn't have 'Wildlife Hospital' stamped on it and there were dozens of cats in the area which liked to leave little mouse parcels around.

This was getting ridiculous. Why should anybody want to persecute a wildlife hospital? It had now been cleared on two separate surprise visits by health inspectors, there was no smell, no nuisance whatsoever and it was no secret that we had been doing the same work for the previous six years without even the whisper of a complaint. I did not want any aggravation; all I wanted was to offer any help I could give to the bleeding, battered and bewildered animals and birds that were brought to me. I decided to put up a six-foot wooden fence to enclose the garden completely.

No sooner had I put up my fence then another six foot fence appeared next to it. There were then three fences between me and my new neighbour's garden so I took my two down and used them elsewhere. What could have been a good neighbourly friendship had evaporated behind a Berlin wall. We never heard from our new neighbours face to face again. I had animals and birds to look after. I hadn't time to go into whys and wherefores, but I could guess what it was all about.

We were becoming more and more *au fait* with the media and were getting to know quite a few of the local radio stations, particularly Radio Oxford and Chiltern Radio. Their appeals to the public were instant and, dealing with wildlife, we sometimes needed immediate action and response. Take the case of the Manx shearwaters. From 1984, each September saw these ocean-going birds crash-landing in

Another shearwater arrived.

the furrowed fields of Buckinghamshire, en route from their breeding burrows around the cliffs of Britain to the coastal waters off Brazil. They were then unable to take off from terra firma. My priority, when they were brought, uninjured, to the Hospital, was to get them back to the sea as soon as possible before they ran into difficulties with fungal disease or thiamine deficiency due to a white fish diet. The trouble was that they never landed all at the same time and no sooner had our friends, Val and John Tyson, who were going on holiday, taken one for release on the coast than another came in. Philip Dunn and Roy Collins, who have been so helpful throughout the life of the Trust, were also going to the coast but I forgot to tell them that shearwaters are diving birds, apt to disappear as soon as they touch the sea. Apparently, Philip nearly went in after his sunken shearwater and was only saved from a ducking when it re-appeared some yards off shore.

Another shearwater arrived. We had run out of people we knew who were going on holiday. The answer seemed to be an SOS put out by local radio stations for willing couriers going near any coast of southern Britain, which is the general direction to Brazil from Aylesbury. The phone began to ring immediately and not only did one bird go to Cornwall but the next was carried to the sea off Portsmouth and both of them sailed safely west into the sunset. Every September we have an influx of shearwaters, although this year there was only one – which Tom and Peggy Cooper kindly placed onto Southampton Water for me.

We had heard no more from the Health Department but the next broadside hit us in November. Our anonymous complainant had approached the Council's Planning Department who then said we were contravening planning regulations and would have to cease operating by February, just a few months away. As usual I could not be told the source of the faceless accusations but once again the media came in on their white chargers and discovered the accusers' identity.

I was never going to let anything happen to the animals and birds which, while they were ill, had nowhere else to go. I made contingency plans to barricade myself in. It was, after all, my house, my

Puffin Billy sends an SOS

PLEASE HELP ME BUY A HOSPITAL

BILLY the puffin landed on his feet when he was nursed back to health after being hit by a car on the M4. Now he is broadcasting a plea to help save his rescuers, the Wildlife Hospital run by Sue and Les Stocker in the garden of their home at Pemberton Close, Aylesbury, Buckinghamshire. They need new premises because a neighbour's complaints mean the hospital must close and £3,000 has already been donated.

castle, which had protected me all those years ago and it was now going to protect those animals.

Then we discovered that, without our knowledge, Nigel Brock, one of our neighbours, the only one overlooking our garden, had combined with Jim Chambers, who lived opposite, and prepared a petition to protect our Hospital. Tirelessly the pair of them knocked on every door in the surrounding streets and almost everybody signed. This was such a wonderful boost to our morale for, although we had lived there for six years, we hadn't got to know very many of the neighbours.

Nigel personally presented the petition to the chairman of the Planning Committee and the Council chose to think again.

Meanwhile, with Philip Dunn's guidance, we had found out how the planning regulations worked and that we were entitled to cover fifty per cent of our garden with any sort of wooden structure we liked – the ground area taken up by our pens and aviaries was well under this amount.

We felt reasonably confident of a simple solution and invited every councillor to come and see for themselves. Most of them did and most remarked that they could not understand what all the fuss was about. In fact the Council came up with the simplest of solutions. They suggested we accept temporary planning permission, to prevent the situation recurring. I maintained that we did not need planning consent but Philip, forever the diplomat, recommended that we accept, albeit with reservations, for the time being.

Since then we have had many dealings with Aylesbury Vale District Council and have always found the councillors most helpful. We have become more and more involved in community affairs, coming out from behind our six-foot fence and making our tiny facilities available for schools and youth groups and in particular for the brave children from Stoke Mandeville Hospital's spinal injuries unit, which is just under the railway bridge at the end of the road.

Two or three times a year we are visited by the same little bunch of children, all confined to wheelchairs but all full of spirit and delight at seeing and touching some of the animals. Young Luke has been coming over for a number of years. A typical East-Ender, he must have been only four years old on his first visit. Too young to sit in a wheelchair the little fellow had to stand in his means of transport. However, this did not damp his spirit. 'I want to see the 'edgehogs,' he demanded, as he was carried in through the back gate. We showed him birds and badgers but no, he wanted to see the 'edgehogs. He had obviously not seen a hedgehog in his native East End of London and was fascinated by the little prickly animals. At last, holding one, he demanded, 'What's that bit 'anging down?' 'That's its tail,' I replied, to which he retorted, 'Oh, I thought it was his willy.' Luke had that natural Cockney ability to keep us all in stitches throughout his visit.

Sue and Luke.

They regularly wear us out as we accompany them back to the Hospital, with races around the track of the Sports Stadium, but that first visit ended with a snowball fight in the Hospital grounds, so that it was a group of tired, soaking but happy children whom we returned to the ward sister who frowned only a little bit at the state of them. We, too, were exhausted and soaked through but wouldn't have missed the experience for the world. Every year now we all look forward to the children's visits and wonder what little gems Luke has got up his sleeve this time.

After that it's very hard to feel down about anything, though the problem with the planning department had soured our work, making us want to move as soon as possible. It was then that we found out about Joe Eggleton's piece of land at Tring. In spite of all the assurances we'd been given, it had after all been earmarked for development, and we were sad, not just at losing a possible site for the Hospital but also at the thought of the bulldozers destroying, without conscience, those priceless specimen trees. Still, Luke and his friends have taught us that it is possible to overcome any setback and, although we realised then it would take a few more years, we strengthened our resolve to find somewhere where, at last, the Hospital could live forever without the prejudices or pecuniary whims of others having any effect on it.

Hook, Line and Similar

As we catered for more casualties from all corners of Britain we found ourselves having to deviate from our prime concern of dealing with sick or injured wild animals and birds, to become involved in pressing ecological issues which were either being completely ignored or else refuted with all manner of smoke-screen lies. We all buried our heads in the sand when the birds of prey were dying off in the nineteen fifties; only when man himself was threatened was any action taken. I was beginning to see blinkered reactions all around when it came to the wildlife welfare. Birds and animals were suffering and dying needlessly when just a modicum of forethought or a mite of legislation could have made so much difference.

Take, for instance, the inept legislation concerning the use of lead as fishing weights. First of all there was a voluntary ban, then a ban only on their sale and a resolution by some water authorities to ban its use. But they are still very much in use elsewhere: the Government 'wets' have acceded again no doubt to the pressure from angling lobby. It's not the boats on rivers which cause lead pollution; it's not the kids on their fishing trips; it's not the weights left on the bank from previous seasons. If you do not believe that lead poisoning from angler's weights causes deaths in water birds, let me tell you of a series of events which rained disrepute on all anglers, not just on

those few who really could not care less.

Each year there is a closed season for coarse fishing when the fish, and incidentally most wildlife, have a chance to reproduce and replace the numbers lost in the previous year and winter. During this closed season the number of swans, poisoned by lead, drops dramatically, proving without doubt that lead poisoning is predominantly caused by angler's weights, recently used and lost. However the principal hazard, left by some anglers, is the imperishable monofilament line which festoon almost every bush, branch and bank of any busy angling area. This never sinks into the mud and only disappears when some hapless bird either becomes entangled in it or swallows it, hook and all, when trying to take the wriggling bait, so often left temptingly there.

I am very tolerant of angling, in fact I was a fisherman myself, once, though I never managed to catch anything. But in 1985, when the new fishing season was barely four days old, an angler brought in to me 400 grams of downy cygnet dying the limp, wasted death of lead poisoning. It could not even lift its head to squeak forlornly for its mother. It was nearly dead but I hoped that the vets might be able to keep it alive long enough for us to attack the lead poisoning.

Tucking the pathetic little bundle under my jacket I went to Tuckett and Gray's surgery, looking for some help but hoping for a miracle. It wasn't to be. An X-ray confirmed the presence of lead weights in the gizzard but in spite of an injection of EDTA, a chelating agent used to precipitate lead from the bloodstream, we all knew it was too late and the cygnet was going to die.

Holding that ball of fluff to me as I drove, one-handed, back to the Hospital, my initial despair turned to hostility towards the perpetrators of this crime. The swan had known less than three weeks of life and here it was, away from its family, alone, perhaps in pain and certainly dying.

By the time I reached the bottom of the High Street I was seething for revenge. The local newspaper offices were just across the road. It was about time, I raged, that the local people were told how their nature reserve, the reservoir where this swan had lived, was nothing of the kind – merely a cover for angling.

400 grams of dying cygnet.

The editor of the *Bucks Advertiser* and his staff were as devastated as we were and promised to do everything in their power to publicise the horrors of thoughtless angling. They took a quick photograph before I made a dash back to the Hospital to make the bird comfortable before it died. It seemed to respond slightly to being snuggled up on a bed of soft towels in a warm hospital cage, but it could not even lift its head and had to be helped to drink a few sips of Lectade, an electrolyte replacement that would give it some strength. We made a high pillow for its head and when it finally succumbed during the night at least its tiny head was held high.

It died only hours before one of its brothers, or sisters, was also brought in, already dead. Even smaller than the first cygnet this bird had apparently been found dead on the 9th June and kept frozen just in case a post mortem was needed. There was no need for a post mortem. I could tell just by looking at the tiny corpse, whose neck was held rigid and right to its back, that it had a fishing hook and line embedded in its oesophagus. My fears were confirmed when I forced open its soft beak to find a fishing line wrapped around its now black tongue and disappearing into its throat.

I knew that both cygnets had died long lingering deaths caused by discarded fishing tackle, but would anybody believe me or, more important, would the anglers believe me? I had recently attended a very informative lecture on the problems facing swans, given by Jane Sears of the prestigious Edward Grey Institute of Field Ornithology at Oxford. Under the directorship of Dr Chris Perrins the Institute had, for some time, been carrying out field research into swan populations and had amassed volumes of vital information concerned with lead poisoning, its causes and incidence. Jane, at her lecture, had said she could carry out post mortems on any swan casualties and she readily agreed to work on the two corpses we had.

The post mortem results were straight from Edgar Allan Poe: our first cygnet's growth had been severely stunted by the five pieces of lead shot trapped in its gizzard. It had virtually no muscles whatsoever: no wonder it could not lift its head. But as if that were not enough to murder it, there was also a mass of coarse fishing line, matted with vegetation, choking its oesophagus and effectively starving the bird.

ANGLERS have been accused of "wholesale slaughter" after lead weights and fishing line killed four cygnets at a local reservoir.

by IAN FLETCHER

hospital lost the battle to save it.

An autopsy carried out at the Edward Gray Institute at Oxford shows that the cygnet had swallowed five lead fishing weights which

not swallowed any weights but starved to death when weed became stuck on nylon fishing line in its throat.

Tests on a third dead cygnet revealed a fishing hook and line in its

"When you see this young, defenceless thing it makes you choke, especially when you think of what it would have grown into. It's not much of a life, is it?" he said.

Now the Stockers are to launch a clean-up

Similarly the smaller cygnet had suffered the long, lingering death of starvation also caused by a mass of fishing line and vegetation blocking its oesophagus and gizzard. There were no lead weights in this bird: it had not had time enough alive to swallow any.

But the massacre was not over. Henry Mayer-Gross, the bushy-whiskered ornithologist who knows every bird on Weston Turville Reservoir, had heard of another cygnet which had died during its first week of life and been buried alongside the only water it had ever known. Gruesome though it might be, we knew we had to exhume that tiny body, if only to compound our evidence that members of the Angling Club, the only people to fish on the water, could be guilty of gross negligence in discarding fishing tackle.

There were no fishing-free stretches of water anywhere near Aylesbury, there was nowhere safe for any water bird and, as the Weston Turville Reservoir was designated a 'nature reserve' by its wardens, the Bucks, Berks and Oxfordshire Naturalists Trust, and only leased to one fishing club, then surely we had enough evidence for them to withdraw the angling rights and give the birds a chance.

However, I cannot see that any wildlife will ever have a chance on this 'nature reserve' which is typical of so many of our national nature reserves managed by the county trusts and used as covers for hunting, shooting and fishing.

Henry, with his veterinary training, and I carried out the post mortem with Barry Keen, the chief photographer for the *Bucks Herald*, recording the grisly results for the public to see. As we opened up that tiny neck the inevitable glared out at us. The same mass of fishing line wrapped around the tongue and entwined with vegetation taken in as the bird had vainly tried to eat. In amongst the great blockage that had, once again, starved the victim were two time-bomb lead shots which would have killed it, anyway, sooner or later. To add to all this, another horror of careless angling now glinted menacingly from the soft pink of the oesophagus: a vicious barbed hook had embedded itself irretrievably inside the bird adding another excruciating pain to the torture already being inflicted until the long, lingering death finally brought relief.

The two resident swans had hatched six cygnets originally but now they had only three left. We knew they were safe from predators and human interference as the male swan, the cob, was feared locally as a tyrant who would unhesitatingly storm out of the water, wings erect, to attack anything or anybody who dared venture near his family. But within five days of our receiving the first cygnet, the cob fell victim to lead weights, too. Henry carried into the Hospital a huge white bundle of skin and bone, a limp, almost lifeless, pathetic shadow of a once proud swan which now could not even stand and had to suffer the ignominy of being carried like a baby.

An X-ray showed the lethal white spots of lead shot in the gizzard where the bird's own metabolism had been slowly grinding the poisonous salts into its bloodstream, bones and muscles. Swans, like all other birds, do not possess teeth but in order to break down their food, which is often stringy vegetation, they deliberately swallow quantities of grit which lodges in the gizzard, an organ below the stomach or proventriculus, where muscular action utilises it to grind the food into digestible particles. Any lead weights swallowed accidentally as grit or on fishing line remain in the gizzard until the

The two remaining cygnets waiting for their X-rays.

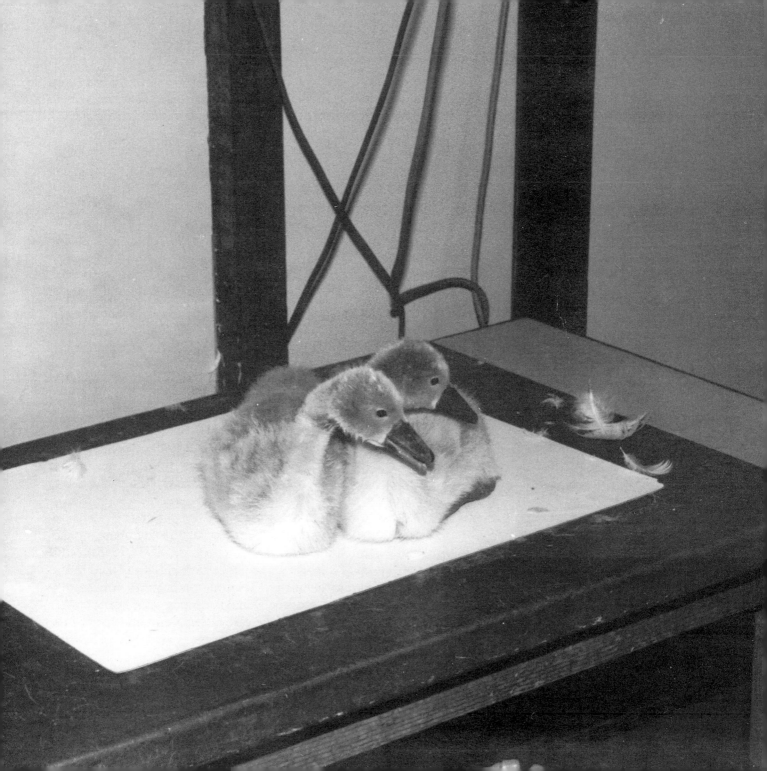

muscular action ensures they are ground away to nothing and have been totally absorbed. Even more horrifying is that two pieces of lead shot can totally incapacitate a bird as large and powerful as this swan, which now lay helpless on the floor of Intensive Care.

The *Bucks Advertiser* and *Bucks Herald* had followed the train of events and, being as horrified as we were, had given over a whole front page to the dilemma at the reservoir. Being fair they also extracted a quote from the National Association of Specialist Anglers disclaiming any involvement in swan deaths and pointing out that the swan population in Britain had increased by seven per cent over the last ten years. Presumably what they meant by this was that one or two cygnets out of every fifteen hatched had managed to survive. Why is it that, in this country, everybody is obsessed with figures? Few of the national bodies seem to care any longer about cruelty. Doesn't the National Association of Specialist Anglers realise that fishing line wrapped around the tongue, or a hook tearing at the oesophagus or slow starvation are all painful and needless torture?

As it was, the lone female swan was left to bring up her remaining three cygnets without the protection of her mate. Of course, the inevitable happened and within days another cygnet had disappeared. Fearing that it might be lying in reeds or on the banks of the reservoir we organised a search party in the hope of finding it alive. We combed and paddled around every inch of the water's edge but all we came across was an angler who challenged our right to be there. He was not very popular and quickly reeled in his line and fled. We had to assume that the missing baby was dead and we were becoming deeply concerned for the three pathetic remnants of the family. They went on sailing serenely around the reservoir, still calling for the cob, but sixty per cent of their family had been destroyed by discarded fishing tackle within the last three weeks and I could only assume that they too would succumb before very long.

I do not usually intervene in the case of apparently healthy birds but this time I felt that I really had no option. As I have said before, the Weston Turville Reservoir is the privileged domain of the angler and to put a boat on the water, especially one with an outboard motor, was tantamount to sacrilege but it had to be done.

We were the proud possessors of a brand new rescue boat bought for us by the British Petroleum Company but I never could master its idiosyncrasies and when I was at the helm it seemed to have a mind of its own and would head for the nearest overhanging thorn bush. Andy Walton, the stalwart of our rescue team, on the other hand, had mastered the ways of outboard motors and was always duty tiller-man. Once on the reservoir, Derek was to be in the prow of the boat as a catcher, while Nigel Brock took up station at likely escape routes on the bank. I had on my new chest-high waders and would lay ambush in the shallows in case the swans came my way.

Sounds easy, doesn't it? A high-powered boat, various large nets and four able-bodied men pitting their wits against three birds. And easy it was to scoop up the pitifully squeaking cygnets. The female was another matter entirely.

She had one major advantage over us, she could fly. As soon as Andy and Derek approached in the boat she would switch to second gear, run across the water, flapping those enormous wings, then engage top gear and lift magnificently into the air, before turning and

'Rescuer One' out to save swans.

flying back over their heads to settle fifty yards astern of them. Three or four times she left the boat and its crew gasping in her wake. To cut down the stress factor, for us as well as the swan, we would obviously have to change our tactics.

All this time Nigel and I had been standing helpless by the bank, shouting out encouragement and, I must confess, chiacking them at each pass. Perhaps, we thought, if I stood in the reeds, in my cumbrous waders, Andy could gently guide her in my direction so that I might be able to grab her as she passed. However, this swan was a master of timing and always at the last possible moment would sail away in the opposite direction, leaving me nearly overbalancing as I tried to pursue her.

I remembered too well how difficult it was, when I had first bought the waders, to walk in them on dry land. In water the effect was comical since I was in great danger of falling over unless I progressed with the utmost caution and much waving of arms. Obviously, after the third attempt, these tactics weren't going to work. Another ploy was needed.

If the reeds had been thick enough I could have remained hidden until she was in range but there was no cover anywhere more than twelve inches above the water. The answer seemed to be to crouch as low as possible to the surface behind the densest clump of reeds hoping she would not spot me.

Andy drove to the other end of the reservoir to herd her towards me again. As soon as I saw her turn in my direction, I ducked behind the reeds to the limit of my waders. I could not see her but could hear the gradual approaching 'phut, phut' of the outboard motor. I crouched a little lower and the first trickles of ice cold reservoir found their way into the top of my waders, creeping down the length of my legs to my feet. The noise grew louder as the trickles became a steady flow but I dared not move. Then I saw her, about three feet away. She saw me and headed for the bank, but I was up on my feet and made a run, or rather a 'dive', for her. I grabbed a wing as I belly-flopped into the muddy water. I had her fast. My waders were by then full of water and I could hardly stand up. But I wasn't far from the bank and was able to pass the bird to Nigel as I made another belly flop. Rather

than attempt to stand up I crawled through the water, to the bank, doing another belly flop, this time onto dry land. Fortunately most of the water gushed out as I collapsed on the ground in my own pool of mud.

As the water ran out I fully expected a small shoal of fish to be left floundering on the bank just as they always do in Tom and Jerry cartoons. Mind you, watching me trying to get those waders off was even funnier than a cartoon. Andy and Nigel finally had to take a leg each and heave the rubber from my sodden clothing. By the time we made our way back to the Hospital we had all managed to sit in the mud and I needed a change of clothing before I could take my latest three swans down to the vet's.

X-rays do not always give a complete picture of a problem but these three were explicit enough to sanction our catching of the pen and her two surviving cygnets. The pen's X-ray showed numerous pieces of lead in her gizzard, together with a recently taken larger weight which, on its own, was enough to kill her. The first cygnet, no bigger than my hand, had three pieces of lead in its gizzard and was obviously suffering from a severe stunting of its growth. Like its mother, it would have died within a few days. The remaining cygnet should have been dead already. Still only a few weeks old it had so many pieces of lead in its gizzard that it was impossible to count them. As if this were not enough to kill the poor bird, it was also carrying no less than four fish hooks in its digestive system. There was absolutely no way of ever operating to remove them and the vet had seriously to consider putting the cygnet to sleep.

For the time being I took the three birds back to the Hospital before we made any ultimate decision about their future. The swans themselves decided the course of action for, as I put the pen onto the patio, still in her carrying bag, the dying cob, lying there covered in a blanket, suddenly came to life and actually hobbled over to his lost mate, greeting her with soft whistles and much swaying of the head. The cygnets saw their father as I carried them through and their gurgles of recognition told me that I just had to do something to save them.

At our open day in April I had met, for the first time, Rorke

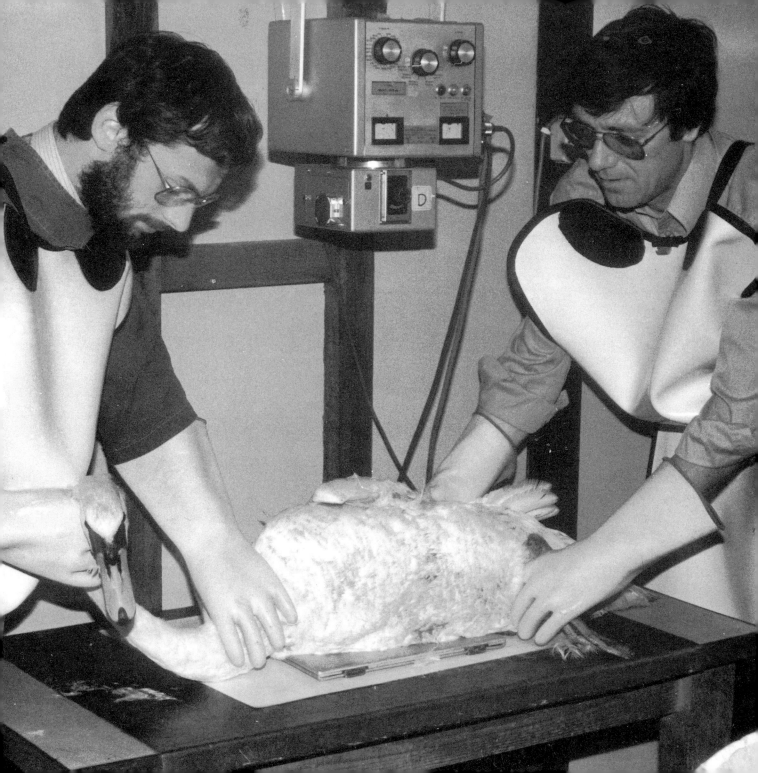

Garfield, a powerful man actively involved in all kinds of animal rescue work. He had told me of a new way of coping with lead poisoning and offered to come down to Aylesbury to demonstrate the techniques. It was the right time to take him up on his offer and, although he is a very busy man, he was on our doorstep first thing the following morning.

He spent all day with us as together we flushed the lead out of the birds' gizzards with 120 mls of warm water. Then we instigated a regime of tube-feeding each swan on a mixture of Complan and Lectade, a procedure used in many American bird hospitals and known as 'gavage', unfortunately after that disgusting French habit of force-feeding geese for *pâté de foie gras*.

For two weeks I tube-fed the adult birds once a day and the two cygnets three times daily. The unremovable hooks in 'Blue' cygnet, as he was known by the blue ring on his leg, would either pass through to be destroyed in his gizzard or else would, we hoped, be calloused over by the birds's natural defence system. The two adult birds also had rings on their legs and from the information stamped on them we were able to establish that the male was a staggering eighteen years old and his mate only slightly younger. As swans mate for life it seemed all the more sad to think that one of them might die, then, after all that time.

The flushing and tube-feeding coupled with daily injections of antibiotics and EDTA were working. All four birds were a lot stronger and eating well, although we still had to keep a close watch on the two adults in case any deep-seated lead residues brought further problems.

But they did not and one month after that heart-warming reunion at the Hospital, the family were fit enough to release on a private pond behind the home of our friends Roger and Jean Jefcoate, who would keep an eye on them.

Once they had been released, fully fit again, Jane Sears managed to get the results of the blood tests on the pen and her two remaining cygnets. The acceptable level of lead is 40 micrograms per 100 millilitres of blood. The pen showed 220 micrograms per 100 millilitres, the 'Yellow' ringed cygnet 1,613 micrograms and little

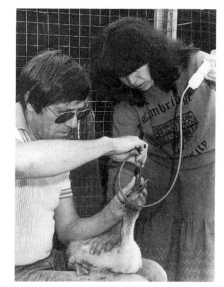

The cygnets had to be tube-fed three times daily.

Les with vet Chris Troughton, about to X-ray a swan.

'Blue', with all his fish hooks, showed an incredible 2,272 micrograms per 100 millilitres when the absolutely fatal level is 500 micrograms. I am glad these figures arrived after we had treated the swans otherwise 'Blue' might never have left the vet's surgery.

Incidentally, this method of treatment for lead poisoning has now been superseded by the use of innovative surgical equipment, but at the time the old-fashioned method worked and I will always be grateful to Rorke for helping me to save those swans.

The family were fit for release on a private pond.

Big Bertha, a Car and a Council

Swans are enormous, brilliant white birds which could not hide even if they wanted to. We never have any trouble spotting a casualty and need only resolve and no fear of getting wet in order to catch one. We pride ourselves on always 'getting our animal', if it is still there to be caught. However, sometimes the larger, more resilient mammals manage, even when severely injured, to drag themselves off and disappear into their environment, probably to die of their wounds.

Typically, on a warm summer morning in July 1985 I received a call from a lady who had been walking her red setter in the woods near to her home at The Lee, a little village not far from Aylesbury. Forever sniffing out every new smell and animal, the setter hesitatingly came upon a large badger lying a under a holly bush. Mrs Johnson at once pulled her dog away but strangely the badger made no movement either to attack or to flee. Tying her dog to a nearby tree Mrs Johnson gingerly crept closer to the badger only to recoil at the horrific wounds on its neck and rump already moving, in the warm July sun, with battalions of flies and their obscene larvae. The badger still made no attempt to move and was obviously in serious trouble, so Mrs Johnson rushed home and phoned us.

As usual I dropped everything and drove, as fast as I could, to the wood which was only about six miles away. Mrs Johnson was waiting by her front gate and led me straight away to the holly bush where she

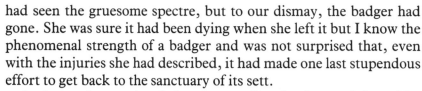

had seen the gruesome spectre, but to our dismay, the badger had gone. She was sure it had been dying when she left it but I know the phenomenal strength of a badger and was not surprised that, even with the injuries she had described, it had made one last stupendous effort to get back to the sanctuary of its sett.

A thorough search of the surrounding bushes and brambles revealed nothing so I set off to search in the general direction of the only known sett in that wood. The day was gloriously warm as I broke into every clump of undergrowth and hawthorn bush, throwing up fluttering clusters of speckled wood butterflies and chattering wrens, getting scratched to pieces by the thorns and bitten by the midges for my trouble. Still no sign of the badger; even my tracking prowess on muddy paths revealed not even a footprint. I found some old woodmen's huts but, prodding around underneath, only brought forth a couple of voles and a disgruntled matriarchal toad.

The undergrowth changed to very tall grass with small islands of hawthorn or holly barricaded with nettles. Every one had to be investigated but there was still no badger, not even the hint of one. The day was getting hotter and hotter; I had the usual bottle of American cream soda to quench my thirst but the badger, if it was still around, must have been suffering terribly from the heat.

By lunchtime I had almost given up hope of finding it and thought it could not survive much longer in the sweltering heat. I could go and round up a posse of willing volunteers but no amount of searchers could possibly cover every nook and cranny in that wood. It might have made it back to the sett. We would be there for days never knowing when to give up. What I needed was a really good bloodhound, like those used in all the best Sherlock Holmes movies.

I knew that friends of ours, Keith Bradbury and Steve Carter, who worked as Rangers for the Forestry Commission, kept small border terriers with reputations as large as bloodhounds for tracking dogs lost by strollers in the woods and forests of southern England.

Steve agreed to meet Sue and me at the wood. He was so proud of his sprightly terrier, Hawk, who was no bigger than our own little Cavalier spaniel Poppy and not a bit like the tracking dog you would expect for an impossible job like this one. For one thing, he had a

very short snout – not much good for smelling with, I thought – small, curled over ears and little spindly legs which looked as if they would surely give out in the thick, tangled undergrowth of the wood. Hawk proved me wrong on all counts and at Steve's command dived into the thickest bush and was soon lapping up every scent and sound the wood could offer. It was obvious at once that no larger dog could have made any headway against the tangled mass which Hawk quartered so vigorously and efficiently.

Steve kept calling encouragement but Hawk needed none of it, rejoicing in his element, his little tail helicoptering in sheer pleasure. We soon lost sight of him and had to follow blindly his frantic rustling until within ten minutes he disappeared out of earshot, funnily enough in the direction of the sett where I had so vainly searched that morning. Steve was getting worried that Hawk might find the badger and fearlessly, as was his nature, approach too close to those jaws which might still be lethal. Or Hawk might even be headstrong enough to venture into the sett where other badgers could inflict serious injury on the game little terrier.

Steve continued to worry and I was beginning to think that Hawk was lost when a frantic barking erupted about three hundred yards in front of us. The grass was too high for us to see anything but Steve knew his dog. 'He's found it,' he shouted, and ran forward leapfrogging the stumps of tall grass. We followed blindly, losing sight of Sue as the grass got taller. Hawk's barking was nearer and Steve, first on the scene, found him jumping up and down on his tiny legs, barking furiously at an innocent-looking clump of grass. 'There's your badger,' said Steve, as he slipped a collar and lead onto Hawk.

'Where?' I asked, still doubting Hawk's prowess. He proved me wrong again for, as I delved, with a stick, into the clump of grass Steve indicated, there in a sorry state was my badger, weak and with very little fight left in it. Just enough to struggle slightly as I manhandled it into the carrying basket. Hawk was now for me the most marvellous dog in the world. He had achieved in fifteen minutes what I had not been able to manage in a whole morning. He thoroughly deserved the fuss Steve was making of him and had fully converted me to the border terrier club.

ACTION

Food chart for baby mammals

Hedgehogs: goat's milk and colostrum (wean onto WHT Glop)

Squirrels: Esbilac (USA) (wean onto digestive biscuits and apple)

Deer: goat's milk (wean onto dandelion leaves and chopped apple)

Foxes: goat's milk (wean onto tinned dog food)

Badgers: goat's milk (wean onto tinned dog food)

Rabbits, Hares: goat's milk (wean onto dandelion leaves)

Mice, Voles: goat's milk (wean onto crumbled digestive biscuit)

Seals and **Otters** are specialised feeders and should be referred to an expert

The badger was very heavy and a bit of a struggle to carry back to the car where I immediately dusted her wounds with Negasunt powder to make a start at killing off all those maggots. I then had a close look at the injuries, finding that, although they were horribly infected and covered large areas of her body (the badger was a female), they were relatively shallow. I hate to say it but the wounds were typically those caused by dogs, presumably in a badger-baiting incident in which numerous dogs are pitted relentlessly against one badger. One of the horrors of badger baiting, so aptly described in a book, *The Working Terrier*, tells how 'Badgers survived weeks of this mindless torture and brutality [baiting] before pining away and dying [not of blood loss but] of sepsis and internal bruising': the condition of this unfortunate badger. It is true that badgers do bite each other in territorial disputes but I doubted whether the injuries would be anywhere near as extensive as those on this animal. Surely no one animal, not even another badger, could have inflicted such wounds on this, a very large badger in her own right? In fact Dr Stephen Harris assures me that he has often seen two badgers indulge in a horrendous brawl only to 'shake hands' afterwards and return side by side to the same sett to lick their wounds. This is not an uncommon occurrence in the natural world, usually signifying the establishment of a 'pecking order' rather than a genuine fight intended to result in serious injury or death.

This badger, whom we named Big Bertha because of her size, had been almost killed by her antagonists and had somehow managed to escape only to be further threatened by the shock, infection and maggots which were near to delivering the '*coup de grace*'. I quickly swabbed the wounds at the Hospital before taking her down to Russell Kilshaw at Tuckett and Gray's, whom we now rely on to see all casualties which need veterinary attention.

Bertha was semi-comatose so, before attempting to work on her wounds, Russell put her on an intravenous drip of dextrose and saline to correct her severe dehydration. He doubted whether she would live but knew he had to remove all the maggots which escaped my Negasunt bombardment by burrowing under the skin. The next hour Russell described as cleaning, debriding and cobbling the

Another badger release.

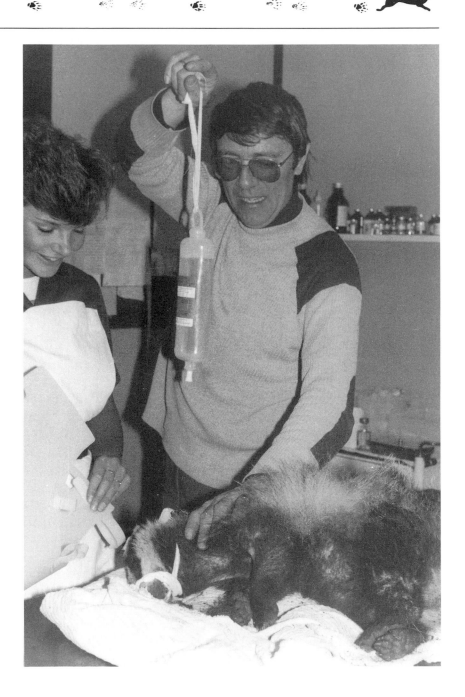

Russell put Bonny onto an intravenous drip.

infected wounds, while I would call his deft suturing, making a patchwork quilt out of the few bits of skin remaining around the large, new raw red patches. He even had to cut into the good skin in places where the maggots had burrowed their way out of sight. At the end of the hour she looked clean and, although in some pain after coming out of the anaesthetic, she looked brighter. The fluid therapy was working, all we could do was to wait while she recovered in the intensive care kennels next to the dogs and cats which were also in-patients at Russell's practice.

The following morning we arrived to find her feeling much better and keeping the nurses at bay. As expected she had destroyed her drip assembly, having managed to get it wrapped around her front

Bonny was barely clinging onto life.

legs. This is where I get called to hold her and guard what Russell calls the 'sharp end', while he removes the remains of her drip and generally checks her stitches. She looks good, at last giving me a good struggle as I hang on to her.

Back at the Hospital I kept her initially in my specially built badger box, six feet long and made of thick timber, so that each day I could run the gauntlet of her jaws to inject her with antibiotics and to try to keep those wounds clean. She was obviously frightened. She could not know that I was trying to help her, and each confrontation became more and more traumatic for both of us. I even invested in a long-reach hypodermic syringe-holder to ease the encounters but on the first occasion that I tried to use it she snapped it like matchwood. Her wounds were still sore yet I had to treat them, an interference she rejected most vehemently. Can you blame her? Time after time she would spin on me, defying me to touch her, making me more than a little nervous of our daily sessions. Eventually I resorted to using the Dermisol multi-cleansing solution bottle like a water pistol, squirting it into Bertha's wounds from a distance, an expensive, wasteful business at ten pounds per bottle, but a necessary one.

However, the daily skirmishes started to pay off and almost imperceptibly the wounds which Russell had not been able to stitch began to close. She no longer needed antibiotic injections and could be moved to an outside pen where she would have more room to keep herself clean and to lick off all that expensive Dermisol that I was still having to apply.

Before I ever took in my first badger, Charlie Norris had warned me that I could never keep a badger in our existing pens. Heeding his advice I had reinforced the walls, only to find that badgers could escape through the top. A reinforced top, as well, only meant that they dug their way out below. Finally I have an impregnable fortress of heavy gauge wire set on a concrete base. I know badgers need to dig but their stay with us is usually only temporary and the concrete base prevents me from having to retrieve casualties from various depths between here and Australia. The only inconvenience of this new badger pen is the small doorway which forces me to bend almost double when getting in or out.

As I moved Bertha to the outside pen she took the opportunity, as I was carrying her through the small door, of turning and clamping her jaws onto my plimsoll, narrowly missing my little toe. Her teeth had no trouble in passing right through the canvas and rubber and locking onto each other. I nearly fell backwards out of the pen, both hands holding her at full stretch while I hopped around the garden trying to make her release her hold on my left foot. I think she was getting her revenge for all the times I had squirted her or injected her, and she would not let go. There was nothing for it but to relinquish my 'plimmy' and dump her in the pen, still gnashing her prize, while I got my now unguarded foot out of the way. When you deal closely with wildlife you are constantly learning and this ridiculous incident taught me never ever again to wear soft shoes while with a badger or, for that matter, with a fox. I was very lucky not to have lost one or two toes in a moment's lack of concentration.

Some weeks and goodness knows how many bottles of Dermisol later, Bertha was looking fit enough for release. I knew she had been found in that wood at The Lee but I could not be sure she would be safe there. Possibly her sett was earmarked by the baiters and could be attacked again, or other badgers could have taken it over. If we could release her into a brand new sett in a protected area, she would have the best chance of rebuilding her shattered life and perhaps even of finding herself a mate.

As it was, fate took a hand when an ideal spouse, a large boar badger, was found and needed treatment at the Hospital. Usually we try to return road casualties to their own territories but this badger, Brock, had a doubtful history which gave us no idea of exactly where he had been found.

First, though, we had to go through the whole traumatic rigmarole of diagnosing his injuries and then, of course, trying to get him fit once more. At first, because he could not use his back legs, we suspected that he had broken his back. However, an X-ray soon proved otherwise and Russell diagnosed damage to the nerves of his legs with a very doubtful prognosis. Brock had other ideas and, although somewhat clumsily, he was soon able to move his legs and half-dragged, half-walked himself around the badger box.

Two more weeks of close confinement proved enough for him to become quite mobile and ready to meet his intended. It's always a dangerous moment when two badgers meet for the first time, and I stood nervously nearby to separate them if they should fight, but Brock and Bertha took to each other immediately. It was as though they had not seen a friendly face for months although even Bertha had been with us for only a matter of weeks. True, they did grunt and snort at each other for a few minutes but they were soon cuddled up together in true badger fashion, in Bertha's box of hay.

To introduce a pair of badgers into a new sett would give them both a fair chance of settling there and making a go of it. But there was better to come. A third member of our ready-made badger family turned up via the RSPCA Inspector from Croydon in Surrey. This one was a small cub, Bonny, who like Brock had been the victim of a road traffic accident. A vet in Croydon had treated her for a punctured lung but even then, when she was brought to us, she was barely clinging onto life and needed Russell's intravenous fluid therapy to pull her through.

Bertha and Brock welcomed the small addition to their family with no bother whatsoever, contrary to the many stories put about that badgers are aggressive to strange arrivals. Their entwined cuddling bodies during the daylight hours made my picture of domestic badger bliss.

Now all that was necessary was to organise their release. Just north of Aylesbury, Roger and Jean Jefcoate have a few acres of land which gradually they are turning over to conservation projects. In creating a small lake, where we released the swan family, Roger had used the excavated earth to cover an old water tank and by leaving an entrance and an exit had in fact created a man-made badger sett overlooked by the kitchen window. It would be ideal for our small family, especially as Roger would also monitor their comings and goings and protect them from interference.

I am forever complaining that too many well-intentioned organisations put most injured animals out of their misery without ever giving them a chance to recover. Bertha would surely have been destroyed, had somebody else taken her in and yet here she was ready to go back

to the wild. I could see that it would be worthwhile taking this opportunity to show the world that wildlife casualties respond very quickly to treatment and can be released to fill their niche in the countryside. So I invited all the press and media to the release, although I took them by coach from the Hospital to the site in order to keep its location a secret until the last minute.

At the same time we were due to receive two very generous donations to the Trust: a new 4-wheel drive vehicle from the British Petroleum Company and Toyota, together with a specially constructed deer-carrying trailer from Rochin Services of Tring. To show our appreciation of the generosity of these three companies I proposed to transport the three badgers, now in individual carrying cages, right up to the sett entrance. Colin Baker, possibly the most popular Doctor Who of all time and a great helper with the Trust's work, would be there to receive the vehicle and trailer officially on our behalf and, on a misty November day, four months after that search for Bertha in the wood at The Lee, everybody was there to see the badgers into their new home.

Laying a scent trail up to the entrance of the sett.

I thought I had prepared the site well, having lined the run-up to the sett with corrugated iron sheets and laid a scent trail of the family's old bedding up to the entrance. I decided to let Bonny go in first. I took her out of her cage and showed her the scent trail. She knew where she had to go and galloped in the right direction, only to bang her nose on the edge of the entrance turning her full tilt towards the people watching from the rear. I thought I had all the exits covered but forgot the brand new car beneath which she scuttled, escaping the enclosure under a gate and rushing headlong for the road behind Roger's house. Andy and I set off in pursuit while Lana shouted warnings to the onlookers not to try to catch the now panicking badger. We fairly leapfrogged the gate just in time to see Bonny disappearing under a hedge. I grabbed her tail, a sure way to get bitten, and pulled her quickly back onto the grass holding her there with a stick while Andy slipped the grasper over her head. Now the embarrassment hit me and I had doubts about having such an open release in the first place, a concern which still haunts me. But the people there appreciated my letting them see the badgers and

Andy had slipped the grasper over Bonny's head.

The Press and media were invited to the release.

were all relieved that Andy and I had caught Bonny, whom I now put directly into the sett entrance. She scuttled into the darkness closely followed by Brock who walked quite leisurely from his cage to the tunnel. I was not going to give Big Bertha a chance to run in the wrong direction and renewed my skirmishing acquaintance with her as I lifted her bodily to make sure she followed the other two into their new home.

As I have said, Roger and Jean's kitchen window overlooked the sett and during the next few months I received regular reports on the family's progress. Although they did in fact move, after two weeks, to a nearby empty sett, the prefabricated mound had served admirably as the badgers' launch pad into freedom and, though I still cringe at the thought of Bonny's dash under the car, I now firmly realise that man-made setts are often the only way to guarantee a badger's safe transition from captivity to freedom.

However, Stefan Ormrod of the RSPCA misread the report of Bertha's rescue in our magazine *Bright Eyes* and accused us of negligently releasing her back into the woods where she was found which, incidentally, are at least twenty miles away from the actual release site.

On top of this misconception, Stefan wrote an article for BBC *Wildlife* magazine questioning the whole concept and value of wildlife rescue and treatment in this country. Our phone lines at the Hospital were soon jammed with outraged readers and rescue centres deeply concerned that the RSPCA, the supposed forerunners in animal welfare, could possibly question the importance of saving an animal's life.

By then I had so much resolve to protect the wild animals and birds of this country that I went to great lengths to refute his criticism and his general attitude that wildlife care involved a bunch of well-meaning amateurs causing more distress in their efforts to help wild animals and birds. It all came to a head in a direct confrontation between Stefan and me on BBC Radio 4's 'Woman's Hour'. Fearing the worst we met on air and, funnily enough, found that, although disagreeing on some points, we agreed on others. The outcome may have been a less heated discussion than the BBC had wanted but our 'head to head' opened doors and minds to a more organised network of wildlife rescue.

We had further meetings, eventually culminating in the birth of the British Wildlife Rehabilitation Council made up of people from the forefront of wildlife concern and the veterinary field. Now firmly established as a crucial part of Britain's conservation strategy, the Council operates purely as an advisory body, but has already broken new ground in arranging wildlife rehabilitation symposia and, at last, getting all the small and large centres together round the discussion table.

★

As a postscript to this chapter, we have just heard that Bonny, the young badger released at the Jefcoates, has now returned to the man-made sett, after eighteen months, and is the proud mother of a healthy pair of badger cubs.

Sometimes You Should Not Let Them Go

I imagine that, by now, you are feeling overwhelmed by stories of my badgers, but, as I come into contact with more and more of them, I become more and more entranced by the animal and its way of living. Quite unlike most other British wild animals, which have all learned to adapt to man's incursions, the badger seems to have ignored us, as though we still do not exist in the same world. Its attitude to every complication is simply to walk through it, head down, oblivious to all around, exactly as it did all those thousands of years ago when the ice caps receded.

Badgers are members of the family Mustelids but, unlike their slimline cousins – the stoats, weasels, polecats, martens and otters – they have adopted a less active, non-hunting roly-poly existence, simply bulldozing their way through life and eating anything that does not need to be chased to be caught.

Man, to his detriment, has decimated most of the other mustelids, yet every time I have a weasel or a stoat at the Hospital I wonder why these most beautiful, symmetrical animals have been labelled for so long as 'vermin' when they, along with foxes, are the most adept at controlling rat populations. The wild spirit of these smaller animals shines out of them. They do not ignore man like the badgers; instead, they defy his giant presence. Believe me, to be spat at by a six-inch

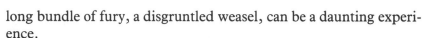

long bundle of fury, a disgruntled weasel, can be a daunting experience.

Not satisfied with destroying all our native hunting mustelids, man then decided to further upset the ecology by either accidentally or intentionally introducing a new member of the family to an empty niche in the British countryside. This animal, the mink, is the equivalent of an enormous weasel and has the same ferocity; but, unlike the weasel, it has no natural enemies to control it in this country. Luckily, in spite of thoughtless mass releases where mink hordes threatened to eliminate all other wildlife, the balance of nature seems to have restored itself, restricting the numbers to suit the habitat and prey availability. Unfortunately one long-term effect of those releases has been to give new life to the doomed otter hunts, giving them a glorious excuse once again to devastate rivers and banks in search of this new quarry. This massive habitat disturbance deters the otter from returning to its previous haunts, while the mink itself is brutally torn to death by dogs. Do not let any huntsman of fox or mink tell you that theirs is a quick, humane death. It is not. Also, I would not mind better that any other animal, including an otter unlucky enough to be caught in the mayhem, would also be torn apart in the frenzy of blood and hunting horns.

Even I had been hoodwinked by the evil reputation of the mink. That was until one was brought into the Hospital, where he left an indelible mark on everybody who met him. This mink had been taking advantage of man's bounty, having set up home next door to a mink supermarket, a trout farm. Dicing with death on every foray, he inevitably, but somewhat fortunately, got himself trapped in a nearby garden, enabling us to send in a rescue team – this time Terry Holder and Don Tremlett, who were no doubt reluctant to test its reputation. However, with caution as the better part of valour, they dropped a bucket over the mink, slid a tray underneath and brought him, just like that, to the Hospital.

My caution was even more pronounced than Terry and Don's, as I put on a thick pair of welder's gloves to transfer the mink from the bucket into a carrying basket so that I could check him over, from a distance, for any injury. What a splendid animal he was! Just like a

Minkie is often the star.

large ferret but with a deep black glossy coat, a white bib and the cutest of faces, set off with bright black button eyes and a formidable set of glistening white teeth. It's not difficult to see why some women try to simulate the beauty of this animal by wearing its skin, but if it were not for their vanity this mink would have been in its rightful habitat in the vast cold forests of north America.

Now all he could hope for was a comfortable life in a cage. He was not injured but I would only be compounding the stupidity of others if I were to release him into our unsuspecting countryside. I had a reasonable-sized wired pen that would have to do for the time being, until I could build him something larger or eventually find him a good home with more facilities to cater for a captive animal – and I wasn't thinking of a mink farm.

Minkie enchanted everyone who saw him and in the year or more that he was with us he never made any attempt to bite anyone. He became a great favourite with all our team of helpers, especially Trevor, who would spend hours feeding him little tit-bits through the wire mesh of his pen. When the television cameras filmed Susan

Hampshire opening our St Tiggywinkles Hedgehog Unit, they took as much footage of Minkie frolicking in his washing-up bowl bath as they did of the hedgehogs eating their dog food. He has now moved to a better home, but during his time with us he gave us hours of enjoyment, especially when the occasional visiting mink-coat owner met her first live mink and realised with horror that she had been wearing the skin of such a beautiful animal.

Until we finally found him a home, Minkie became one of our small accumulation of permanent residents. This is a quite unintentional collection of animals and birds which cannot for one reason or another be released. Our garden and garage space at Pemberton Close had been perfectly adequate when we moved in but the shortage of space really kept us on our toes and made sure that we released as many of our patients as possible.

However, sometimes opening the cardboard box reveals an animal or bird with injuries far too severe for it ever again to be resourceful enough to return to the wild. If this situation arises, we try to keep the disabled animal in as natural an environment as possible for the rest of its natural life or until we can find it a good caring home with similar resources. We pride ourselves that we never put an animal down just because it cannot fly or is lame in one leg. Each year we can still vividly remember and count on one hand the casualties that have to be put to sleep, predominantly as the result of broken backs or the loss of two or more limbs. Every one involves a lengthy evaluation by Russell and myself and, if an animal has even the slightest possibility of recovery, it is given the benefit of the doubt and a chance to survive.

Most patients, even some with horrific injuries, which are brought in to us, make a perfectly good recovery. The one affliction for which we have no cure is that of being tame. Whenever the cardboard box discloses a tame bird or animal, we know from the outset that it could never survive in the wild and can never be released.

The crow family are probably the easiest of all birds to tame, and the cute but ugly babies are also some of the easiest birds to raise by hand. But in the process they so easily become imprinted on their foster parents. Not too bad, you might imagine, except that the

condition is irreversible and the cute, ugly baby will soon grow into a handsome but very large, powerful, messy and destructive full-grown corvid which has no place in the house. Our first experience was with a carrion crow, one of the largest of the family, which had obviously been taken from the nest and hand-fed at his every beck and call. Call was certainly the operative word. We could hear him even before we opened his cardboard box, cawing for attention. And a crow's caw is surely the most ear-shattering of all bird calls, especially when it's right on your own doorstep.

He came out of the box, mouth open, pink gape yawing, shouting his vociferous demands, I think, to the whole of Aylesbury. I stuffed food into the gaping, pink cavern in the vain hope of quietening him down but he still managed a choking caw as the food went down and, without stopping to take a breath, he was at once demanding more. They say that to teach any animal its adopted name you have to repeat it constantly, so it was no wonder that this unfortunate bird became christened 'Shut-up'. Even when he was confined in the garage his

Shut-up, the crow.

insatiable demands could still be heard inside the house. In an aviary with other crows I hoped he might find himself a mother. But no such luck. As nuisances go, he was outstanding. Most birds sleep at night but not Shut-up. I had only to touch the handle of the back door, even in pitch darkness, and he would start his cacophony. It's a wonder that he did not wake half the neighbours. Then, one day, he escaped and with mixed feelings of horror tinged with relief, I went out to look for him. I found him without any trouble. He had flown only as far as Nigel's garden next door and was gleefully pulling the pegs off the washing line, letting the washing fall to the ground. I sneaked in and grabbed him before anyone else saw his little misdemeanour.

He had to go. It was a 'me or him' situation, but I could not just throw him out – it would not have been fair on him, or the world at large. Luckily, Sue thought of somebody who might take him as a pet. A couple in High Wycombe had a pet rook which lived in an aviary in their garden and Sue remembered they were looking for another bird to keep it company. Shut-up would make an ideal companion and I knew that he would have all the attention he could possibly demand.

Peace reigned on the day he left, although he was still calling like a ventriloquist's dummy from the confines of his cardboard box. Apparently, he gave up his incessant cawing when he met his new aviary mate. Instead, he would give a perfect imitation of Sue calling the dogs in at the Hospital, followed by a perfect rendition of Poppy's bark.

All the crow family can learn to talk if they hear the words often enough and the next corvid we took in was already a past master at just two words when he arrived. Maggie was a magpie which had somewhere learnt to say 'Go 'way'. Yet, unlike Shut-up, he was very choosy as to whom he would talk to. He would not talk to me or Sue but would have a repetitive conversation with only specific visitors. Needless to say, at the first sign of a television camera or a microphone he would shut up like a clam, although he could not resist going through all his other tricks like collecting 10 pence pieces, or tweaking Poppy's tail if she passed too close to his aviary. His

Maggie would have a repetitive conversation with specific visitors.

A flying visit to dismantle Les's chess board.

intelligence was annoying in the world of bird-brains and he even learnt to undo the bolts on his aviary door, making a flying visit to the house to dismantle my chess board before disappearing over nearby houses.

I searched but gave him up for lost, hoping that with his wit he might somehow be able to eke out an existence in the wild. But his tameness and lack of survival techniques dragged even Maggie down and eight weeks later, when I was called to a magpie holed-up in a garden shed on the other side of town, I knew from the 'Go 'way' as I caught him up that it was he. He looked terrible: feathers all bedraggled and his tail broken, but Maggie was always a constant bather and ten days later was once again the exceedingly handsome cheeky sprite he had always been. The amazing thing about seeing birds at close quarters is that none of them look remotely like the facsimiles you see in bird books. I had always thought that magpies were black and white, but really their dark feathers are a shade of lustrous dark blue-green. Maggie was a prime example of magpie colouring except when he moulted and then he became completely

bald-headed, giving visitors, I am sure, the impression that he was not doing too well.

The reality was quite the contrary. Maggie was the complete master of every aviary I ever put him in. His intelligence was phenomenal; I never knew any other bird, even other crows, to get the better of him. But Maggie had one failing: he was a committed bully and would attack any other bird, regardless of its size. I do not know how many times I have had to rescue a much larger crow or rook from his clutches, but Maggie was always on top shouting 'Go 'way, go 'way' at the victim pinned to the ground beneath him. Eventually I ran out of aviaries and had to look for alternative accommodation for our problem character. I arranged to take him to Stagsden Bird Gardens where his non-stop antics could keep the visitors amused. I need not have worried about leaving him in a new, strange environment, for as we left we could hear the resident magpie telling Maggie of its experiences while all Maggie could say in reply was the inevitable 'Go 'way'.

Before we condemn all corvid orphans as unraisable, I would like to say that if the job is done properly without allowing the birds to imprint onto humans, then it is possible to release the bird and for it to lead a perfectly normal life.

★

In spite of Minkie's and Maggie's stage presence it was still the constant influx of injured hedgehogs which captured the public's and the media's imagination. And of course when Minkie and Maggie had moved out, the journalists could give their undivided attention to the plight of our prickly patients. Hedgehogs are unmoved by limelight and, although most of our other patients were kept away from the cameras, the six or seven hundred hedgehogs looked after each year gave ample scope for filming without giving stress to any individual animal.

All the television work was done at the Hospital and recorded, giving opportunities to edit out or re-take any mistakes, but the day eventually arrived when Thames Television asked Sue if she and a couple of hedgehogs would feature on the first transmission of the new children's magazine programme, 'Splash', which was to be live.

We were both handsomely entertained at Teddington Lock studios and, while I sat back minding the hedgehogs, Sue spent most of the day rehearsing. All went well until ten minutes before transmission time when suddenly all the presenters were missing. Sue innocently asked where they were only to be told that they were in their dressing rooms doing their Level A breathing exercises to overcome their nerves. Until then Sue had been fine, but this news set her butterflies a-fluttering and set me walking her round the car park while she did her own Level A. She felt better within minutes and was on time, waiting in the wings for her cue. On camera just before her entrance was one of her heart throbs, David Cassidy, who as he came off gave Sue a reassuring cuddle, adding the words 'There's nothing to worry about, Sue. After all there are only six million people watching.' Surprisingly, Sue found strength in this but really I think it was the cuddle which saved the day. The cue came, Sue took up her position with the hedgehogs and everything went perfectly. Nowadays Sue has no worries about live television but only, I am sure, because each time she imagines his being there with her.

It seemed as though the whole world had been waiting for someone to start caring for hedgehogs and, as soon as we opened St Tiggy-winkles in 1985, the world's press and television wanted to know about our work. We even had a television team from Australia come to film the hedgehogs, although there are none in that country, but the programme was also broadcast in New Zealand, bringing us sacks full of mail about their hedgehogs which are, after all, direct descendants of British ancestors released there during the last century.

Television was making people aware of wildlife casualties. Our next involvement was behind the cameras as a direct result of an appeal put out by Wincey Willis during her weather bulletin broadcasts on TV-AM's 'Good Morning Britain'. I must confess to not being an avid breakfast television viewer, so it was Margaret Mortham who heard Wincey tell how, on feeding the ducks and moorhens on Camden Lock, next to the studio, she had noticed that one of the moorhens had its foot entangled in deadly monofilament fishing line.

Hedgehogs prepare for their TV debut.

Wincey has facilities to rescue injured birds at her home in the north of England but in London had no way of helping the moorhen. She asked for a local group to help out and catch the bird so that it could be treated. Until then I had been unaware of Wincey's deep concern for animals and birds but, as soon as I phoned the studio, she went out of her way to give us all the support imaginable in our efforts to rescue the 'Camden Coot' as he had become known to viewers.

The only drawback was that Wincey regularly fed the birds at four-thirty in the morning, when we would have the best chance of catching the casualty. Sue, Andy and I would have to get up in the middle of the night to have any chance of success.

With the boat strapped to the top of the car and nets, boots and motor inside we sped through London and in no time at all we were pulling into the car park at the peculiar building that houses TV-AM's studios at Camden Lock. Wincey had arranged a car parking space under the building close to the canal and, to Andy's delight, next to Roland Rat's Ratmobile. The terrace onto the canal outside the canteen was where Wincey fed the birds but, as is usual with wildlife, the moorhen we wanted did not turn up for its breakfast. Andy and I would have to search both ways, up and down the canal, until we could find it and work out a strategy for catching it. The problems started there. The terrace on which we were standing stopped at the end of the building. The only towpath was on the other side of the canal and there was no way of getting over other than by launching the boat and paddling across.

Once ashore we split up, with Andy searching upstream, above the two locks, and me going down below the pool outside the studios. We now have two-way radios for this type of situation but then, if we spotted the bird, we had to retrace our steps and try to signal to the other party. This time it was Andy who was the lucky one. I heard him calling in the distance and could see him running back in my direction.

He had spotted a moorhen with a lame foot about half a mile upstream just where the canal widened out into a vast basin. We would need the boat but would need to carry it up past both the locks so we decided not to take the outboard motor. We could come back

for it, if necessary. As it was we had to paddle back over to fetch the nets and catching equipment from the car and, by the time we had carried everything up to the basin, we were already out of breath.

All through these preliminaries Wincey was flitting in and out, giving her weather bulletins to the nation as well as updates on the 'rescue of the Camden Coot'. I only wished we felt as confident. Moorhens have a tremendous repertoire of escape tactics, including swimming, flying and diving. The only talent this one lacked was being able to run, yet his other skills enabled him to lead us a merry dance, which culminated in our being led into a dark, sinister underground lagoon littered with dead and decaying boats, a black, horrible place ideal for hiding bodies or other horrors. In the depths of this cavern the water seemed to become shallower, so our strategy was to herd the moorhen in that direction and, at the last moment before we ran aground, I would leap into the water and trap him on dry land. Perfect planning but nobody had told the moorhen which, when cornered, simply took off and flew low over our heads back to daylight and the open canal basin.

We turned and charged after it as fast as Andy could paddle. It had swum in amongst some moored barges, an ideal place for me to creep up on it from above. Gingerly I landed on the first barge and crept across two of them until I spotted it nonchalantly bobbing along the channel between them and the bank. However, it had spotted me first and made like a submarine, diving out of sight, to resurface about twenty feet away en route once more for the gloomy cavern.

Once again we followed it in, watched it fly over us and back to the barges. Three times we made this trip, with Andy doing all the paddling. We had to try a new strategy. If we were to give this elusive moorhen an obvious flight path out of the cavern keeping him between the boat and wall I might well be able to butterfly-net him in mid-air. Gently Andy paddled behind the moorhen once more, all the time veering slightly to the right, encouraging the moorhen to go to the left, towards the wall. We were stationed less than eight feet from the wall as he jumped up to a niche in the brickwork. He had only one escape route, down our port side. He dived towards the open water behind us. I had the whole channel covered and before he could change direction I had swept the net into his flight path and had him. In the gloom I thought we had better check that we had the right bird. Yes, there it was: the mass of fishing line and lead weights cutting into his leg and foot. All we had to do then was carry the boat and the equipment back to the studios, this time with a wriggling wet moorhen up my jumper – I had forgotten to take a carrying basket.

Sue and Wincey were waiting on the opposite bank and let out a great cheer as I produced the bird from my clothing. It was nearly nine o'clock. Wincey had just one more weather bulletin to present and could show the viewing millions that we had safely caught the 'Camden Coot'. However, the moorhen had other ideas and, once in the studio, managed to escape from Wincey's grasp just before they were due to go on air and made off amongst the cameras.

I took some of the fishing line off while at Camden Lock but the bird was going to need a course of antibiotics so we took it back to the Hospital with us.

The moorhen's foot reminds me of the old townie pigeon I spotted while waiting for a train on Marylebone station. The bird had cotton wound around and cutting into its feet so, as nonchalantly as possible, I scattered some biscuit by my feet and, when it approached near enough, grabbed it round the shoulders. Everybody on the station looked at me as though I was mad but when I showed them all the cotton and my trusty penknife. they thought I was a hero. But the cotton had bitten very deeply into the foot and, as I unwound it, the pigeon started to bleed profusely, as birds' feet always do.

Quickly I wrapped my handkerchief around the foot to try to hide the carnage. A nearby cardboard box served as a carrying case to bring the pigeon back on the train to Aylesbury for treatment, but I wonder what my audience thought I was up to. Have you ever had that feeling when you wished the ground would *really* open up and swallow you?

Like the pigeon, the moorhen responded well to treatment and, although it lost one of its toes, it was soon back at Camden Lock greeting Wincey at that unearthly hour every morning when she braved the elements to feed the birds.

Wincey Willis shows the 'Camden Coot' to viewers.

One added bonus to our encounters with the Camden Coot has been that Wincey, ever since, has been a firm friend and become Vice President of the Hospital, never hesitating to do all she can to support any of our projects. And when the firm of Kiddicraft asked her to propose an animal charity which could make use of a large promotional plastic spider, Wincey put us forward. The arrangements were that Sue and I would meet Wincey at the Toy Fair, where she was launching her new weather game, to receive Webster the spider on behalf of the Trust. Robin Bennett from Kiddicraft was there to meet us and so was Webster, suspended in the centre of Earls Court – the largest spider I had ever seen. Robin told us that it had cost thousands of pounds to build and measured fifteen feet across the wheels. Yes, it had wheels instead of feet, weighed in at four hundredweight and cost two hundred pounds to erect each time it made an appearance. Webster was a wonderful character which completely captured the hearts of Aylesbury when it made its next appearance at our second open day, suspended high above the stage at Aylesbury Civic Centre. At the moment it is still lying in its lair, special storage at Slough, waiting for the right moment to take up residence at our new hospital complex, but that's another story altogether . . .

At about this time we received a phone call, out of the blue, from an old friend of ours, Rob Clarke, whom I had known since my days as a member of the Aylesbury Round Table. Very successful in the property development field, Rob had been responsible for creating one of the most pleasant estates in Aylesbury and was then proposing a prestigious housing and leisure complex on very poor farm land just north of the town. An integral part of the plan was to create a twenty-seven acre angling-free lake, conservation areas and a children's zoo. However, Rob suddenly thought of an alternative to the zoo: he would donate some land on which to build the wildlife hospital I had always dreamed about. At last it looked as if we had found a permanent home for the Hospital after all those years of searching and disappointment. I could take in even more casualties; I could have an oiled-bird unit; Biddy and Granny could have their own sett; the deer could have convalescent paddocks: the ideas were

Webster the spider.

circling around in my head. There were so many things I wanted to do and the generosity of Rob and his company, the Royco Corporation, were about to make it all possible.

However, one snag continued to worry me. I was concerned that we might find ourselves tagged as a 'zoo' when it is the one thing we strive not to be. We would be an amenity to the town but I could not foresee us opening our doors for visits from the general public. We had to make sure that we remained, first and foremost, a wildlife hospital offering medical facilities to wild animals and birds, and a social service to relieve the good people who stop to pick up casualties and have nowhere else to take them. Our third goal was to create a wildlife teaching hospital, the first of its kind in Europe, where like-minded people could come and see the work we were doing, learn some of our techniques, as we would learn theirs, and perhaps go away to set up their own wildlife hospitals throughout the country. This is the only way Britain can possibly hope to cope with the millions of wildlife casualties that at the moment are left to die, unattended, just because there are no other facilities to give them help.

Now, please do not take my rejection of zoo status as entering into the argument for or against them. It's just that most of our patients are unused to the close proximity of humans and constant public access would be exceedingly detrimental to their convalescence and rehabilitation.

That's not to say that I do not sometimes have zoo animals brought into the hospital. There were the two Indian pythons and the steady stream of terrapins but perhaps the most perplexing was the lizard found in a furniture warehouse in High Wycombe. I have treated our British common lizard on a number of occasions so was not surprised when a telephone caller told me a lizard was on its way. As usual, there was an enormous cardboard box for a tiny animal, so as usual I slid my hand in first, without opening the lid, to catch hold of the lizard before it escaped under the fridge or furniture.

The hissing made me stop and jerk my hand out. That was an almighty sound for four inches of lizard. I decided to take a look before I went in again blindfold. I lifted first one flap of the box and

Les with Komo, the monitor lizard.

then the other. Two great eyes looked up at me and a giant forked tongue flickered out at me. A two-foot-long body stretched out behind: here was a monster lizard and it just as well that I had removed my hand when I did. It was some species of monitor lizard but I did not have to be an eminent zoologist to see that it was all skin and bone and had not eaten for quite some time. But then there is not much in the way of dragon fodder inside a furniture warehouse. How on earth, I wondered, had it got there in the first place? Perhaps it arrived in the country in a piano or, more than like, a bamboo sideboard.

The little dish of flies I had collected in anticipation of a smaller visitor looked rather puny alongside this monster. I would need something far more substantial, preferably not my fingers. I managed to get some locusts from a friend who bred them for an exotic bird collection and Komo, as we called him, loved them, although I was not sure I could stand watching him crunching the large bright green insects leaving their legs and wings poking out from his jaws at all sorts of obscene angles. I thought to try him on a defrosted frozen mouse offered from a gloved hand. He snapped at it more in aggression than recognition and, with some loud crunching, down it went.

From that moment he fed solely on mice and, within two weeks, had put on an enormous amount of weight. He no longer cowered behind his tree but stood in the open waiting for me to drop food into the cage. Then he decided not to bother to wait and the next time I opened the door he was out of it like a rocket taking the mouse and most of the skin from my fingers. He was getting decidedly dangerous and, although I would have liked to keep him, I knew that he would be much better off in the reptile house of one of the national zoos.

I had always been impressed by the conditions at the Cotswold Wildlife Park and had often received a great deal of help with insect diets for odd birds like cuckoos. I had also recently met the keeper of the reptile house while doing a pilot television programme at Weston-super-Mare so I rang them. They said they would be delighted to house Komo and so I arranged for Chris Kirk, who just happened to

be going to the zoo with his parents, to take the monitor along.

Chris was to pick Komo up at nine o'clcock in the morning, on his way. I had not handled the lizard since the day it had come from the warehouse but I was taking no chances: I donned my pair of thick welding gloves before grasping him just behind his front legs. He was no longer the wimp he had been but a very powerful animal and it was quite a struggle to get him into a carrying basket.

It was about an hour's drive to Burford so I was surprised when the Wildlife Park phoned at lunchtime to ask where the monitor was. I assumed Chris must have broken down or made a sightseeing detour into Bourton-on-the-Water or Bibury but when he still had not arrived by four o'clock I was getting deeply worried for his safety. Not from the lizard but from a road accident or something. I phoned Chris's home. No reply and still no reply by five o'clock when the Wildlife Park closed. What could possibly have happened?

I could get no answer all evening and when, bright and early in the morning, Chris turned up with an empty basket, I automatically assumed the worst. The monitor must have escaped and Chris had not wanted to tell me. But the animal could not survive outside in our cold climate. 'Why didn't you phone me?' I demanded.

'Why should I?' he retorted.

'Why should you? Because you can't just let a monitor lizard escape and disappear without mentioning it. That's why.'

'I didn't let the monitor escape. I delivered it just as you told me to,' replied Chris, looking at me as if I had gone mad.

I was getting a little bit incensed by his innocence. 'How come, then, that the Cotswold Wildlife Park kept phoning me to ask where you had got to?'

'Because I delivered it to Whipsnade Zoo, just as arranged.'

It appeared that Whipsnade were coincidentally expecting a Bosc monitor so did not think it strange when Chris turned up.

However, I had a terrible job apologising to Cotswold Wildlife Park for the shenanigans of the previous day and I am not sure that they believed me. Mind you, I am not sure that I believed me either.

Deer, Deer

In spite of our occasional run-in with an exotic species, people were beginning to realise that, at last, here was a wildlife group which actually cared about wildlife. We must have been a revelation to radio and television companies who began flocking to see genuine concern and involvement in wildlife conservation. (Mind you, major organisations like the World Wildlife Fund still insist that looking after wildlife casualties does not constitute conservation.) Britain for too long has lived on its reputation as a nation of animal lovers. The rest of the world is laughing at us, as was epitomised by the Australian Paul Hogan's show where he ridiculed the fact that Britain has more wildlife conservation groups and wildlife reserves than any other country – the only drawback being that we have no wildlife left!

We are now shouting from every platform possible: 'Look to your wild animals and birds before it's too late. Ignore the incredible propaganda that it's only the shooting fraternity who will protect the countryside. Ignore the "put a casualty out of its misery" brigade. Wildlife can be saved but it must be done now.' We are not frightened of over-exposure: the more people who hear our message the better, and unlike some groups we have nothing to hide. The animal comes first, before all other considerations. This is the practical conservation people want to hear about.

By 1987, after nine years our work and recuperating patients were being seen all over the world. When a local newly married couple decided to have a honeymoon in Hawaii, they thought they were getting away from it all, until one morning during breakfast the husband called his wife from the bath to see the couple at St Tiggywinkles saving hedgehogs on Honolulu Television, getting our message over to another audience. We once had dissension amongst our volunteers with a motion to stop all media coverage of the Hospital. For the only time since we have been a registered charity we pulled rank and vetoed such a retrograde step. My reasoning? If all the newspaper articles and television programmes encourage someone, somewhere, to save the life of just one hedgehog, then all the time, bother and inconvenience involved will have been well worth it.

Struggling to cope with the French through a Paris television channel severely tested our resolve to communicate, but perhaps the outcome made a few Europeans more aware of their own native hedgehogs. Travelling to the Lake District to do some filming for Tyne-Tees Children's Television Sue and I had the added attraction of working with David Bellamy, who is so important for the future of Wildlife. Sue had a touch of the flu but I am sure felt much better after David bought her a pint which she could not lift, let alone drink.

It's a long journey back to Aylesbury from the Lake District and, although I know that Nigel and Sharon Brock, who live next door, are more than willing to take in any animal or bird that arrives, I still worry about what casualties are going to turn up while I am away. We arrived back on a gorgeous Saturday afternoon with the tell-tale aroma of barbecuing wafting from the next-door garden. Nigel and Sharon invited us to join them but first Nigel said he had one casualty, in his garage, which perhaps I ought to look at before I started on the wine. Usually it's blackbirds or rabbits or the occasional seagull but this time Nigel warned me, before I blundered into the garage, that there was an adult muntjac running around loose because he had nothing large enough to put it in.

Muntjac deer were introduced to this country at the beginning of the century and since then have spread quite considerably over the central and southern counties. Unlike the three larger species of deer they have no fixed breeding period and are consequently thriving. Their solitary nomadic life style means that unlike the herd-forming species they are not a nuisance and so far have escaped that excuse for shooting, the organised cull. They do, however, have a true deer temperament, tending to go completely berserk in their efforts to escape confinement. Like all deer they have tremendously powerful back legs tipped with sharp hooves, which can severely injure the unwary handler; added to which the bucks have short often sharp antlers and razor-sharp tusks protruding from the top jaw. They use the latter for fighting with other bucks – I have treated a loser with seventy-five cuts on his body. I have also known dogs and their handlers to receive quite large slashing wounds as the result of a run-in with a muntjac buck.

So that was what Nigel had in his garage, and it had to be caught. Apparently, this buck had a broken leg, but even on three legs a muntjac can out-run and out-jump most other mammals, and in a semi-confined space like a garage, he was also capable of causing himself considerable damage in his blind panic to escape. But I have a lot of experience of deer and over the years have used reason and science to perfect an infallible technique of catching them in this type of situation. Of course, to start with you need resolution, and then you grab any bit of the deer you can and hang on for grim death until someone slips a mask over the animal's head to quieten it.

Once the muntjac was under control I put it into a large wire-topped box where, although they have some scope for movement, they tend to remain reasonably docile. At close and quieter quarters I could get a good look at the broken leg. As with all fractures in mammals brought to us, this was a job for Russell's orthopaedic skills and, since wild animals will try to walk on a fracture, it had to be treated as soon as possible. Another Saturday evening spent in the steam-charged atmosphere of the surgery.

We have now mastered the idiosyncrasies of deer anaesthetic so with me acting the nurse and keeping an eye on the deer's breathing, eye reflexes and depth of anaesthesia, Russell was able to work on the fractured metatarsal, reducing the fracture and wrapping the leg before 'popping' it – vet's jargon for applying a plaster of Paris cast.

The cast would have to be changed after a week and at regular intervals for some time afterwards. However, when we removed the second 'pop' after nineteen days there had been severe degeneration of the skin caused by the intense pressure a deer exerts on its hind legs which had pulled the bone fragments apart and some had penetrated the covering skin.

Obviously the pressure was too great for the bone ever to heal so Russell decided that some form of internal fixation was necessary. I know it sounds horrific but by using his practice's newly acquired surgical drill Russell was able to bore into the bone fragments. The pieces were then stabilised with stainless steel lag screws. The problem was then how to cover the operation site when even the small amount of skin a deer has on its legs had suffered from necrosis and infection. I know Russell will not admit it, but he improvised with what skin there was and indulged miraculously in a bit of plastic surgery to make sure there was ample covering round the wound. We did not need another plaster of Paris cast as the two screws were holding the fracture absolutely rigid. A light non-stick dressing and bandage were sufficient to cover the wound but this would need changing in five days' time.

Often, as in this case, the introduction of metal to a fracture is the only course of action but this is also an ideal medium for the introduction of infection and must be monitored very closely. Back at the Hospital Sue and I now had to give the deer a complete course of antibiotic injections in its rump, a procedure any deer objects to. First, I had to catch the deer, which is one of the reasons why I keep them in closely confined boxes so that I have only to grab and hold an antler before lifting it out with my other arm around its middle.

Once I had the deer I would sit on a stool with it across my knees while Sue sought out the muscles in its rump and drove home the injection. At that time I made a practice of holding a deer's hind legs to control its kicking. I now realise that this is not necessary as it would only be kicking air, providing, that is, nobody gets in the way. My attempt to control its tremendously powerful back legs almost destroyed the joint in my elbow and caused me pain for nearly a year afterwards. Another lesson learnt the hard way.

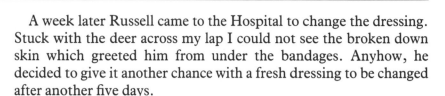

A week later Russell came to the Hospital to change the dressing. Stuck with the deer across my lap I could not see the broken down skin which greeted him from under the bandages. Anyhow, he decided to give it another chance with a fresh dressing to be changed after another five days.

After that period of time there was still no sign of healing and more skin had deteriorated. Russell's strategy would now be to rely on secondary healing, where the body should gradually form new tissue to cover the upper of the two screws which was not fully exposed.

For nearly three weeks Russell made frequent 'house calls' but the deer still showed no sign of healing while my elbows grew steadily more painful from the continual wrenching. I would have carried on until my arms dropped off, but the time came to make a serious decision about this deer's future. The leg was not healing and would probably have to be amputated. Though a tame three-legged deer can live quite happily in captivity, a completely wild adult muntjac buck which could not be released was an absolutely hopeless prospect. It would never settle to the proximity of humans and would in time, no doubt, seriously injure itself in its efforts to regain its freedom. Together, we made the decision to put him to sleep. There was absolutely no other way.

The morning of the execution came and very dejectedly I wrestled with the deer for the last time as I took him down to Russell's surgery. As I held him on the prep room table, neither Russell nor I said a word as Russell drew up the fatal injection of pentobarbitone. Russell and I have been through some traumas and sometimes it's very hard to keep a positive optimistic outlook for wildlife. People sometimes get the wrong idea about us especially when we give animals light-hearted names like 'Tripod' for a three-legged hedgehog, or 'Orange Sauce' for a duck, and call all our foxes Samantha, but I am sure that helps us face moments like this one. 'Let's have a last look at that leg,' suggested Russell: he was clutching at straws and really we both knew it. Gently he cut away the strapping – it's strange how the vet's 'curly' scissors, as I call them, are always blunt. It seemed to take for ages but for the first time there was no putrid smell. Russell fairly tore at the last of the bandage. He had become all

After several weeks the muntjac was walking with only a slight limp.

fingers and thumbs where usually he was so dexterous but at last it was uncovered. The wound was pink and healthy: it had started to heal. Russell is never very demonstrative but I swear I saw him jump in the air and click his heels together in jubilation. This deer was going to get better.

The wound healed and after several weeks the deer was walking with only a slight limp. The amazing thing was that his own natural resources had made that leg grow to twice its normal thickness.

Five months after he had arrived we took Billy, as he had become known, to be released on a private estate. Russell, for once, left his surgery to come with us and was soon clicking away with his camera. It was probably the first time he had actually witnessed the release of one of his deer patients. Usually he only has a chance to photograph the casualties as I take them to his surgery looking much less healthy.

To see a deer run off into the undergrowth gives you an emotional lift never to be forgotten. But working with wildlife casualties is a rollercoaster of emotion: one minute on top of the world, the next in the depths of hopeless despair, with deer near the top of the list for heartbreak. It's not the deer which cause the heartbreak, of course, but their collision with man and his intervention in their environment. Badgers have always ignored man's presence; foxes, for ever living on their wits, have in fact out-mastered humans; but deer are so simple and fragile that at times they just cannot cope. They are always getting themselves into the craziest of predicaments and it hurts me that I cannot always do something to help them.

Take the time I went out with Sue, at nine o'clock one morning, when all my volunteer rescue team were on their way to work and unobtainable, to a fallow buck in trouble. The buck had apparently been trying to leap a fence when it caught one of its back legs in the top of it. This happens fairly frequently and if you get there before the deer dies of a heart attack you can often just cut the wire to release it.

This buck was caught in a fence alongside a busy road next to Pitstone cement works. It must have been there since before dawn.

The moment we arrived I knew were were in trouble. Not only was it a full-grown fallow buck weighing nearly two hundred pounds, but he had his leg trapped not in a wire fence but in a solid metal fence of the type they used to erect around parks. There was no way that I

The fallow buck had his leg caught in a metal fence.

could possibly cut through an inch of solid iron. Looking at the deer I could see that his ankle, jammed in the fence, was obviously broken and his leg twisted up and over his back suggested a dislocated hip, a major problem in a deer who has such a shallow hip joint. There was nothing that I could do. I dare not go near him as I could not possibly restrain him: he was too powerful for three men to hold, let alone just me. There was no way of sedating him for, even if I called Russell out, we could still not get close enough for an injection. Then there were the Forestry Commission Rangers who, if I called them out, would only be able to shoot him, but perhaps in the circumstances that would be the kindest thing. As it was, the buck decided for us. From a standing position he executed a phenomenal vertical leap up and over the fence freeing his injured leg in the process. Dragging the injured leg he galloped into the distance, leaping a thick hedge on the way as though it were not there.

I had seen that the fracture of the ankle had in fact broken the skin and knew that, in no time at all, this would become infected, slowly but surely killing him. We had to try to find him and for a whole week we spent every night out searching the fields and gullies. Keith and Steve came down from the Forestry Commission but, although with their expert field craft we put up many fallow bucks, we never caught a glimpse of our quarry. Until a week later when the police called Steve to a fallow buck lying on a nearby housing estate. As we had feared the infection had taken over and he was beyond help, so Steve did what he had to do, there and then.

The outcome of all this horror and to make sure that never again would we have to stand helplessly by while an animal suffered, was that we urged Russell to obtain clearance from his practice to use a rifle which fired tranquillising darts. My photo of that poor buck swung the argument, and Russell is now trained and fully licensed to handle the dangerous equipment. Touch wood, we have never yet had to call on his expertise and I, for one, would be only too happy never again to find a deer in that predicament.

But not all deer stories are sad ones. The happy endings for Mistletoe and Costly are still like a shot of adrenalin to me.

Mistletoe, as you may have guessed, was a Christmas arrival. Well, she arrived on Boxing Day actually. She was the tiniest of muntjac fawns whose mother had been killed by a car on Christmas Eve. She had been picked up from beside her mother's body and looked after over the holiday by kind people who knowing no better had fed her on bottled cow's milk which can be lethal to deer. By the time she arrived with us, she could no longer stand and, even more worrying, was 'scouring' – the ruminants' equivalent of diarrhoea which kills more cows and sheep than any other single complaint.

Putting her in the warm baby incubator, we immediately tried to bottle-feed her with Lectade to counter the dehydration and restore some of the energy she had lost. We struggled at first because she did not recognise the scent of the new teat on the bottle. However, we long ago learnt the secret of how to get a baby deer to feed. With all mammals it is essential to stimulate them to urinate and defecate either before or after a feed. Deer like it to be done at the same time, so while you hold the bottle at one end, you have to, with a rubber-gloved hand, gently stimulate those sensitive zones at the other end. Mistletoe was soon guzzling away on Lectade although we did have to hold her up on her feet to perform her natural functions. Russell was on duty that weekend and called in to see her and take a photograph, but not until he had given her an injection to ease her intestinal problems.

After twenty-four hours on Lectade, Mistletoe seemed much brighter with her eyes losing that 'on the way out' look. We could now get her gradually onto goat's milk which we find to be an ideal food for most young mammals. Muntjac start browsing at a very early age but another quandary of the introduced species is that in the middle of winter in England there was virtually nothing growing that could be of nourishment to this young deer. Deer are supposed to relish the evergreen leaves of ivy but it did seem rather tough for those tiny jaws. As luck would have it, on the way to our local shops there was a grand crop of fresh chickweed which had escaped the municipal gardener. The trouble was that it did not keep for long once it was picked, so two or three times a day I increased my exercise régime by walking to the shops and, as unobtrusively as possible, grabbing handfuls of chickweed and hastily stuffing them up my jumper.

Mistletoe on goat's milk.

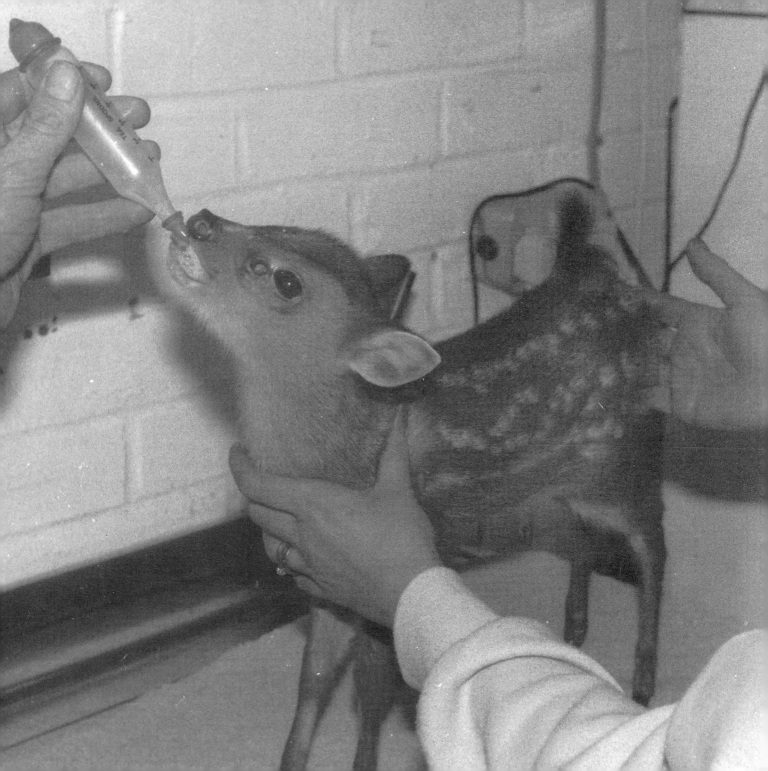

The exercise was worth it and within days Mistletoe's stools took on a more regular shape and the 'scouring' was over. Tottering slightly, she even struggled to her feet, her head almost touching the top of the incubator. We moved her into the wire-topped box where I had kept the muntjac buck, although this time we added a heating element to keep her warm. As well as the continuing bundles of chickweed she was also tucking into chopped apple and pear, which were her absolute favourite. We would soon be able to wean her onto goat mix, the staple diet of all our deer casualties, but for the moment she still loved her bottles of warm goat's milk, giving little squeals of delight as she suckled.

Twelve weeks after her arrival she was quite at home dismantling our garden lawn, and Russell and I had to go on a working trip to America. I say working trip, though many would laugh at my audacity. In fact we were going to a wildlife rehabilitation conference at Clearwater Beach, near Tampa in Florida. When I tell you that we were staying at the Holiday Inn it begins to sound even more like a holiday, but to me it was anything but. I do not like being away from home and cherish the opinion that flying is for the birds. After all, if a world heavyweight boxing champion can have a phobia about going up in an aeroplane, why shouldn't I?

Russell, of course, was looking forward to it and, although neither of us had flown before, he actually wanted to sit and look out of the window. In no time at all the 'No smoking' signs went out and I opened my eyes to find we were way above the clouds. I didn't seem to suffer the vertigo I have when standing on cliffs, but then the lady sitting next to me had discovered free brandy in the galley. The air hostesses didn't look worried but why, I wondered, did Russell keep looking out of that window? At least we were over the Atlantic, so there wasn't much chance of hitting a mountain, and I am sure it was just their little joke to put the 'Fasten seat belts' sign on when we were about halfway across and to bounce us around for fifteen minutes. Then, at last, there was land below. 'Oh, that's bound to be the Bermuda Triangle,' said Russell reassuringly.

We were about to land – I hoped the brakes worked – when there was an announcement: 'No smoking while we are in Miami. We shall

be taking off in about an hour.' Surely we should have been in Tampa? They don't tell you when you buy the tickets that you are going to suffer two take-offs and two landings. However, this time we were barely airborne before the pilot switched off his engines for the glide into our rightful destination of Tampa. I was getting quite blasé about flying and even ventured a look out of Russell's window. We were flying over the vastness of the Everglades, a place I had always dreamed of visiting if only it hadn't involved an aeroplane trip.

At Tampa Di Conger, my American friend, was waiting with a taxi to take us to our hotel. I had expected to get mugged the moment I walked out into the street or mown down in one of those spectacular crashes of black and white wailing police cars, but Clearwater Beach was a pleasant surprise. The moment we set foot on the 'sidewalk', we spotted an enormous brown pelican flying over the road. Russell and I both whipped out our telephotos and ran off half a roll of film each. However, on walking round the block we bumped into dozens of them literally waddling up to take food from our hands. Our hotel

Dozens of pelicans in Florida.

balcony was also within touching distance as the great birds flew from one lagoon to the next and laughing gulls and iridescent grackles quarrelled over tit-bits we threw to them from our hotel room. It should have been a paradise on earth.

As it was, I was in a dream throughout that week, wondering and saying out loud to myself, 'What on earth am I doing here?' Halfway across the world and knowing that I was going to have to fly all the way back home.

The wildlife theme of the conference, and my daily before-dawn calls to Sue got me through the week. In America they truly care for their wildlife casualties. At this conference alone there was representation from over a staggering, seven hundred wildlife rescue centres all across America. However, the highlight of the trip was a short visit to the Suncoast Seabird Sanctuary with the romantic address of Indian Shores, Florida: one incredible acre, crammed amongst the towering luxury hotels, totally geared to the care of injured seabirds in a glorious setting looking directly onto the silver-white beaches of the Gulf of Mexico. They had in for treatment all those species I had dreamed of and seen only in picture books: pelicans, egrets, ospreys, red-tailed hawks and even an anhinga, the legendary snake-bird of the Everglades. This was my element and for a short while I even forgot the impending aeroplane flight back to England.

On the last day we had the opportunity to take time off and visit one of the world's best known tourist attractions. Quite the reverse of Suncoast, it's a revelation in the exploitation of wildlife which goes on under the noses of millions of unseeing people. Sea World boast of its giant killer whale pools and the only baby whale born in captivity. It has the world-famous acrylic tunnel where you are escalated along amongst the sharks, but what you don't see on the posters or on the commercials are the little dried sea horses and puffer fish on sale for pieces of silver, or the saws cut from the front of sawfish. No mention is ever made in the sales pitch of the mighty walruses swimming aimlessly and hopelessly up and down in a pool no bigger than my front room. This was razzamatazz at the expense of living animals, and the only thing which did not disgust me that day was the cup of

Mistletoe walked up to be introduced to Costly.

coffee I drank by the lakeside while watching a wild osprey performing its aerobatics to the unseeing crowd.

My early morning phone call to Sue the following day was supposed to cheer me up but it only increased my resolve to get home. I discovered that the day before Sue had sent Andy and Nigel out on a deer rescue only for them to find another tiny muntjac fawn, this time itself the victim of a hit and run driver. It had obviously suffered severe head damage in the collision but, as Russell was with me in America, Sue had to take 'Costly' to another vet who, lacking Russell's experience, could suggest nothing more than 'wait and see'. In the meantime I was certain that Sue was doing all that could be done, but I wished I could be there too.

At last, two days later, it was time to go. Back to Tampa, the short hop to Miami to pick up a few more passengers then out and over the 'Pond' as Russell calls the Atlantic. Russell went to sleep and stayed that way for hours: at least this meant he could not keep reminding me what was below. Finally, Russell woke up and pointed out the Scilly Isles. The pilot switched off the engines. For half an hour we glided, I'm sure. Then we were there – Heathrow at last. We taxied all round the airport while I decided that if the pilot took off again, I would open the emergency hatch and jump out. At last we stopped. Sue said that, when she met us, I looked as pleased as Punch to be home while Russell looked miserable. Outside in the car park it was cold, damp and drizzling. It was great to be home.

We rushed back to Aylesbury to look at Costly. We were both extremely shocked at the extent of his obvious head injury. His whole head and neck were twisted completely over his right shoulder while his left eye stared upward, sightless and swollen and incapable of being closed. Russell knew immediately what action to take, giving all manner of injections and producing from his little black bag hypromellose drops to keep the eye lubricated.

Costly, unlike Mistletoe, was a little fighter who was a handful if ever he was taken out of his incubator. For the time being we kept him there, feeding him, using the same regime we used for Mistletoe, except that it being later in the year there was a reasonable choice of greenstuff available as well as chickweed.

Buttermilk with her leg in plaster.

He started to grow quickly and was soon too tall for his incubator. He fought like a demon as I wrestled him to the wire-covered box. We knew that he could not see too well but he responded to Sue's voice so she had to spend hours with him coaxing him, stroking him, until at last he settled.

His head was still grotesquely twisted to the side but as Sue regularly manipulated his neck it gradually started to improve. Russell was deeply concerned about the condition of the exposed left eye and in fact stitched the eyelids together to give it a better chance of recovery.

Week after week Costly walked round and round his box, refusing vehemently all our efforts to get him outside. Occasionally, his agoraphobia forgotten for the moment, he would stand on the grass and take a bottle from his beloved Sue. And then one day Mistletoe walked up to be introduced. Here was the mother Costly really wanted, although she was not much bigger than he. From then on he followed her like a lamb and it was Mistletoe, with her constant licking and grooming, who brought him on. She showed him the little shed where they were to live for the next few months and they became inseparable. His head was gradually resuming its natural position, though the eye still showed a massive scar on the cornea. He was, and still is, extremely nervous, but that is probably the result of not being able to see too well.

We could never release them to a fully wild existence as Mistletoe would soon end up in a venison freezer and Costly could never cope with the assault of other muntjac bucks. They are both living on a private estate where they are nurtured and cosseted, and rumour has it that we may soon be hearing the patter of tiny hooves.

*

Yet another muntjac fawn actually arrived at the Hospital in a cardboard box. She had broken her leg and as Russell was plastering it, he asked for a name to put on the record card. The box was labelled 'Linseed oil' and 'Buttermilk', so Buttermilk she became – another one of our silly names. This one remained quite wild, however, and we were able to release her as soon as her leg had healed.

Moonlighting

Deer are generally far too large and boisterous to come in cardboard boxes but you would be amazed at the enormous variety of animals and birds which arrive in an even larger selection of boxes many of which are hardly suitable for their occupants. Perhaps the most outlandish are the gargantuan containers used to transport the minutest of bats. Maybe the superstitious carriers imagine that their winged charges are going to take on human form once it gets dark and the enormous boxes would give them room to metamorphose.

Though the tiny bats are not even related to the vampire bats of America, if you pick one up you may be confronted with an inch of vehement, spitting pipistrelle, baring an impressive row of one millimetre teeth which might just make you reach for the garlic.

We have treated all manner of bats at the Hospital from these tiny courageous pipistrelles to the handsome furry long-eared bats with ears the same length as their bodies. We have had baby bats in liqueur boxes, rare bats in egg boxes and, on more than one occasion, dead bats in ice cream tubs or coffee jars, but they have always been individual casualties, the result of one-off encounters with some hazard or another. However, imagine our consternation when Patty Briggs, an ardent bat-watching friend, brought us two rare Daubentons bats, along with two corpses, the survivors of a massacre of over seventy in the last three months on a solitary patio by the canal at Rickmansworth.

We read of the decimating effect on bat colonies of wood preservatives and other careless chemicals but here was a major disaster, right on our doorstep, needing some smart detective work to find the cause and put a stop to it before any more bats succumbed.

But all that sleuthing would have to wait. At that moment I had in my hands two Daubentons bats which needed urgent attention if they were going to survive their injuries. Perhaps that was our first clue, for it would be unlikely for a poisoned bat to be injured before it died. Although not as tiny as pipistrelles, these two bats were only one and three quarter inches long, making their injuries very difficult to treat. My experience has been that if you can get a bat to feed and drink you might stand a chance of keeping it alive, but if you dive straight in and start to pull the animal about, as you have to even to check its wings, then the odds are that it will die.

One of the bats was particularly weak and, in spite of warmth and a few drips of Lectade into its tiny mouth, it died soon afterwards. The other bat, 'Nora', relished the Lectade and was soon happily lapping

up the 'glop' – the dog food and dried insect concoction which we feed to baby birds and hedgehogs. Nora also ate a few mealworms and, presumably contented, adopted an upside-down position, hanging from the roof of the cage, to groom and clean its fur and the remains of its wings.

Together with the two frozen corpses Patty had brought in, the bat which had died meant that we now had three tiny bodies where investigation through necropsies might give us clues as to their demise. There was some degree of urgency so Russell decided to do a post mortem on only one of the bats leaving the other two for toxicological examination which needed to be carried out at a specialised laboratory. The post mortem, as expected, revealed no obvious causes of death although, as I have said, there were extraordinary signs of traumatic injury. We would need the involvement of Bob Stebbings and Sheila Walsh, the country's renowned bat experts, who apart from maintaining small groups of injured bats also had access to poison investigation procedures. Bob was deeply concerned about the Rickmansworth problem and offered any help we needed, including agreeing to adopt Nora, who could never be released, into his small group of Daubentons.

The bats had all been found on the same patio, which was walled on three sides, so we could assume that the roost was in that precise vicinity either in the cottage itself, in nearby ivy-covered trees or, more than likely, in the depths of a road bridge which hung low over the canal right next to the cottage. Local members of a bat group had more or less quartered the cottage, eliminating that. Since the nearby trees and, of course, the bridge were over the canal itself, we would have to bring out our rescue boat if we wanted to investigate further.

The section of the canal was no longer navigable so to launch *Rescuer One* we had to carry her from the car along the Rickmansworth by-pass, down some treacherously steep steps and over a garden fence. Once on the canal Andy still had to manhandle it over a partly submerged tree, checking for bat roosts as he went. Picking up two members of the bat group he gently paddled under the bridge which they found to be riddled with all manner of likely bat roosts all requiring a very thin arm to investigate them. Patty was at once

One of the surviving Daubentons bats.

volunteered and was soon up to her elbows in potential bat sarcophagi. Somehow the bat experts judged one of the holes to be the elusive roost but Patty could feel no bats. Presumably, if there were any survivors, they were entombed deep in the heart of the concrete honeycomb.

While they were poking and prodding under the bridge I took the opportunity to carry out a full-scale search amongst the bankside trees and ivy cladding. I did not find any live bats but only a partially mummified corpse which the bat-men assured me was a Daubentons. I must say they revelled in the find. They measured it, weighed it, felt it; I only hope they did not get near enough to smell it, but it made their day – at least they had seen a bat.

Using the cottage as our incident room, we all sat around drinking coffee, kindly supplied by the lady of the house, brainstorming the fragments of evidence we already had. But so far the only common denominators were dead bats and the patio. I sat there stroking the cat, clutching at straws: 'What about the cat? Does he go out after dark?'

'Yes.'

'Is it possible that he could sit on one of the overhanging branches and swipe the occasional bat as it passed underneath?'

'Couldn't happen,' retorted our hostess. 'My cat has never caught a bird, let alone a bat.'

'Can we just try something, though? Could you keep your cat in at night for the time being?'

Nobody was really convinced by my theory but it was the only possibility to be put forward. We then had the muscle-wrenching ordeal of carrying the boat back to the car park, but this time I carried the camera and left Nigel and Andy to flex their muscles.

All the way back to Aylesbury we chewed over possible causes of the bat mortalities but until we had the results of the toxicological investigations my cat hypothesis was the best we could come up with.

The following day Sue and I drove to Peterborough to see Bob and Sheila, a chance to discuss many bat problems, not just those of the Rickmansworth Daubentons. Nora was introduced to her home in a new type of bat housing they had designed and which we now use for our bat casualties, finding it eminently suitable for these difficult little patients. Bob also took on the two corpses and would let me know as soon as possible of his findings.

A few days later he phoned me with the report of his investigations which showed no undue poison levels but which highlighted injuries to both bats as typical of those inflicted by a cat. After that, we confirmed that the cat in question is no longer let out at night – and there have been no more Daubentons casualties. Added to which, Sheila has recently written to say that Nora is doing very well in her new home.

★

The launching of the boat and the investigations under the bridge would have made good television footage, but our experience has shown that the only way to make good film is to stage events to suit the camera. Real life is simply too chaotic and unbelievable. We regularly get the chance to show and explain our wildlife work on television and in particular on children's programmes like 'Caterpillar Trail'.

Sue and I love getting involved with 'Caterpillar Trail', not just because Wendy Duggan is an old friend and one of the nicest people we know, but because the Trail is one of the best children's programmes on TV giving, as it does, so much sensible time to the animals of the world. Normally we go into the studios to add our contributions but, as they wanted to cover the release of barn owls into the countryside, we arranged for their cameras to film one of the barns we use for our reintroductions.

The first stage of the filming was at the Hospital showing some of our barn owls due for release and highlighting the male and female we were going to use for this particular project. We were taking the owls up to Sally's farm where dozens of white owls (as they are known to country people) had been released and had bred in the wonderful collection of old barns.

Stuart Bradley, a Vice-president of the Trust, is the regular presenter of 'Caterpillar Trail' and together we were motoring up Sally's drive, with the barn owls on board, for this first on-location shooting, when the heavens opened. We got soaked as we rehearsed, then filmed and then reshot the removal of the owls from the back of the car. We grew even wetter filming our grand entrance into the barn through the quagmire which was by then six inches deep in water. Four or five times the director shouted: 'Cut. Let's do it again!' Eventually we were inside the barn, where various stages of the introduction of the birds – such as putting up a ladder to the nest box, unpacking the boxes and putting the owls in their nest box – were to be filmed separately but to show continuously in the final outcome. Stuart and I were gradually drying out which was no good for continuity, so before each take we had to go outside, stand in the rain and get back to our previously soaked condition. By the close of filming we were soaked and shivering while the rest of the crew were as dry as toast. But it was worth it and Stuart's wonderful humour kept us in fits of laughter throughout the day.

The film was superb, a credit to the crew and the direction. My acting was hardly deserving of an Oscar but it did show to the young viewers the value of practical conservation measures.

For the next television work we went back to the BBC Television Studios, for Sue to do a live appearance on 'Blue Peter'.

Sue was now more confident about once more venturing into live television, this time to show the world Snowflake, the surviving half

Snowflake – the surviving albino hedgehog and star of 'Blue Peter'.

of twin albino hedgehogs which had come into the Hospital from north Buckinghamshire. All through the summer months we take in dozens and dozens of orphaned animals and birds. It might be hundreds more but we do insist that a young animal is not 'rescued' unless it is confirmed beyond reasonable doubt that it has been orphaned. Snowflake was one of a family of five tiny orphan hedgehogs whose mother had been killed in tragic circumstances. The real surprise was that two of the babies were pure albinos, whereas their three brothers and sisters were coloured like any other baby hedgehog.

We were confident that we had mastered the enigmatic art of rearing baby hedgehogs by feeding them colostrum as well as goat's milk for a full six weeks as opposed to the one or two days which is usual for other mammals. However, these five hedgehogs rejected our bottle-feeding and were losing weight at an alarming rate. We even took the drastic measure of worming them and introducing a course of antibiotics, a procedure we would rather not have adopted until they were at least three weeks old. Even this had no effect: we were only just keeping them alive. The smaller of the two albinos was markedly weaker than the other four babies, giving us great concern for his well-being. He was so weak that we were forced to take him away from the others so as to give him extra warmth and subcutaneous fluids to try to stop his decline. All to no avail, for gradually he slipped into a tiny coma and died.

We had worked along with Russell on this family ever since they came in. We also had another family of five tiny black hyper-active hedgehog babies which were also giving us a hard time. No routine medication seemed to have any effect on either family. Could they possibly have a similar infection which had not previously reared its ugly head? As with the Daubentons bats, the only way to discover the cause and to have a chance of saving the others was for Russell to perform a post mortem on the tiny dead albino and perhaps come up with a cure. Unfortunately, it can take forty-eight hours to establish the results of any bacteriological tests but as soon as Russell had even an inkling of the problem he came to the Hospital to institute, as it turned out, a life-saving course of injections.

Prickly issue confronts the Commons

Woman Police Constable Karen Anstiss escorting hedgehogs at the Commons yesterday when they arrived at the invitation of Mr Robert Jones, MP for Hertfordshire West. He handed a 35,000-signature petition calling for better protection for the species to Lord Caithness, Minister of State at the Department of the Environment (Photograph: Peter Trievnor).

PS

TORY MP Robert Jones has picked the best possible team to help him prick the conscience of the Environment Minister, the Earl of Caithness, tomorrow . . . a delegation of 40 hedgehogs, positively bristling with determination.

Wielding a 35,000-signature petition which calls for full legal protection for the hedgehog — it has been raised by the only hedgehog hospital in the world, St Tiggywinkle's at Aylesbury, Buckinghamshire — Jones plans to lead his spiny squad to Parliament Square to press his point.

It's enough to make any tradition-conscious parliamentarian curl up.

I HOPE you will share my pride in a foster son who actually made it to Westminster — and has participated in a demo which could change the law.

You may recall Ben, the young hedgehog who wintered with my family and departed in April for the Wildlife Hospitals Trust at Aylesbury, in Buckinghamshire. Little did I suspect that while Erinaceus europaeus was mulling over his morning chicken drumstick, he was also becoming a politically aware animal.

Apparently, Ben was among a party of 40 hog democrats who demonstrated on the grass of Parliament Square in support of Tory MP Robert Jones' 35,000-name petition calling for the full protection for the species (of hog, not MP).

There was nothing flippant about the request; the survival of one of Britain's most environmentally vital little animals depends upon it getting protection under an appropriate Act of parliament.

Sue and Les Stocker, who run the Trust's hedgehog hospital, were pleased with the dignity and decorum of their 'charges' demo. (Not surprising; hedgehogs are orderly creatures compared with the inmates of the House.) Sue said: "We were very pleased with the reaction we got from people. We have got to get the message all over Britain. Hedgehogs must be protected."

Right on.

In his laboratory investigations he had found that the dead baby had, possibly, pathogenic bacteria in its intestinal tract, which were only susceptible to chloramphenicol, a specific antibiotic that was not generally used as a routine broad spectrum medication. He had confirmed the necessity to administer it but as there are no recommended dose rates for hedgehogs, especially babies, he had to calculate a dose small enough to use but still possible to measure. The minuteness of the dose was mind-boggling even in the small world of hedgehog medicines. Twice a day, we would have to inject 0.02 ml, two-hundredths of a millilitre, intramuscularly into each of the hedgehogs. And it was not a case of just grabbing a hedgehog and jabbing. Each time I had to pull out one tiny back leg, insert the smallest needle we could find into a muscle, aspirate (that is, pull the plunger back to make sure I had not entered a blood vessel) and then push the plunger home. I had to do this twice a day, in alternate legs so as not to cause too much damage. The trouble was that the hedgehogs soon cottoned on to my little tortures and started to practise their rolling-up techniques just to make sure that they prickled me as I stabbed them.

As always with a new course of antibiotics, it was a couple of days before the hedgehogs felt any benefit. Then, all of a sudden, the four hedgehogs were ravenous for food while the five little black ones still kept us on tenterhooks for another two weeks. The original gang of four began to put on weight at last and were soon enjoying first 'glop', with an enzyme additive to aid their digestion, and then great bowls of Pedigree Chum Puppy Food, although Snowflake, with his pink eyes, always shunned the light and would eat only underneath a towel. He is still a very fussy feeder and will eat only after all the lights are out and even then will often turn his nose up at something he has been eating for weeks. We have to bow to his gourmet demands and only Snowflake has specially bought giant mealworms and Mr Dog, the ritziest of all tinned dog foods.

It was Snowflake who was the great star at the launch of *The Complete Hedgehog*, the culmination not just of many years' involvement with hedgehog casualties but also of two years of research into their biology, history and status around the world. The book was

A patient for 'St Ollies'.

launched at Chatto and Windus's offices in Bedford Square, London, with all our Vice-presidents turning up to support this, one of our greatest projects so far. But it was Snowflake, on his first public appearance, who stole the show. Now quite a large hedgehog and definitely Sue's favourite, together they stopped the traffic in Bedford Square as they faced the barrage of the country's press but Snowflake did blot his copybook by taking a nip at Sue's nose during one of those face to face poses the newspapers love.

The launch was a tremendous success and *The Complete Hedgehog* made it to No 2 in *The Sunday Times* bestseller charts, an unheard of occurrence for a book dealing specifically with one type of wild animal, but then that's the charisma of the hedgehog. Sue and I toured the country for dozens of those inquisitions known as book-signings and despite that British Rail advert which asks, 'When did you last see a train with a puncture?' I am sure our sleeper from Edinburgh had one, as it stopped for three hours on an obscure stretch of track somewhere in Cambridgeshire. To make matters worse there was no heating, it was six o'clock in the morning and sharing our tiny sleeping compartment was Patches II who did what all hedgehogs must do, forcing us to flee into the corridor.

The Complete Hedgehog is intended to show all facets of the hedgehogs of the world, with particular stress on their well-being and care if injured. To date over forty thousand copies have been sold. If each person who bought a book saved just one hedgehog, then the equivalent of a third of those killed on Britain's roads each year would be saved.

The train journey was unfortunate, as we had always enjoyed a good relationship with British Rail, with their Red Star service bringing many injured hedgehogs to us in record time. In 1987 they offered us a free extension of the Hedgehog Express by including, for six months at least, injured owls in their ambulance service. Birds have travelled by rail for many years: in fact it was the pigeon-carrying service which first alerted me to the possibility of bringing hedgehogs to Aylesbury. Now we could set up the same rescue service for owls and could start a new wing of the Hospital and could call it . . . St Ollie's, what else?

Red Star to The Wildlife Hospital Aylesbury

Clean any wounds or maggots from animal or bird.

Warm any cold casualty on a covered hot water bottle.

Try to get treatment locally.

Take box to nearest Red Star Parcel office – Monday to Thursday only.

Label box:
WILD ANIMAL
THE WILDLIFE HOSPITAL
AYLESBURY.
PLEASE TELEPHONE ON
ARRIVAL: 437373.

When condition is stable, place casualty, wrapped in towels or hay, in a pet-carrying box and tape the top.

Pay carriage charge, and then phone Aylesbury (0296)–29860 to inform of its departure.

Some Red Star offices may demand a certificate of fitness to travel from your veterinary surgeon.

Do not send young or baby animals by Red Star. Phone the Wildlife Hospital (0296)–29860 for advice.

A much younger Colin with the ichthyosaur bones excavated all those years ago.

We set everything up at the Hospital to receive any number of owls. The press and television arrived, giving untold publicity to Red Star. John Craven came down to film and, even though the hourly train into Aylesbury was fifteen minutes late, the resultant film really showed how a liaison between an animal welfare group and a state industry could work. Or so we thought. The first owl to need the services of British Rail was turned away because the Red Star operator knew nothing of the arrangement. Red Star fees, which when we started with hedgehogs were about £5 per animal, are now nearer £12. But I'm sure the problems can be ironed out and the system be made to work, to save owls and hedgehogs which might otherwise perish.

★

After all this star treatment, it's time to get our feet back on the ground, our new ground to be precise.

The Royco Corporation have now started work on Watermead where we are going to build our new Hospital. Rob Clarke tells us that they have already started excavating the twenty-seven acre lake and are using the resultant spoil to create the dry ski slope which will be right above our complex. Many years ago Sue, Colin and I did some small excavations ourselves in that general area, uncovering the fossilised bones of aquatic dinosaurs which had lived there, in a warm shallow sea, one hundred and fifty million years ago. Ever since Rob had told us about the proposed lake we had been expecting the excavators to reach the Kimmeridge Clay which held these Jurassic fossils. When Rob finally told us they had found dinosaur bones, I am afraid we rather took the wind out of his sails with our casual answer: 'We thought you might.'

Rob still needed access, across the piece of land he had donated to the Trust, for about another twelve months so for the moment all we could do was to stand back and watch the lake, conservation and ski slope take shape. I say 'stand back' though at the Hospital nothing ever stands still and, apart from the enormous support and influx of casualties the hedgehog book had engendered, it also produced a staggering request: I was asked to give a paper to the prestigious British Veterinary Zoological Society at their symposium on hand-

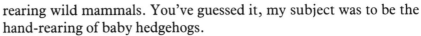

rearing wild mammals. You've guessed it, my subject was to be the hand-rearing of baby hedgehogs.

I was *fairly* confident that we had handled more baby hedgehogs than anybody else and was *fairly* confident of our techniques. Notice my hesitation there. I would not qualify my confidence like that, but my audience was to be made up of some of the top veterinarians in Europe. I prepared my paper well and Russell went through it to correct my veterinary jargon. He came along to give me moral support at London Zoo where the symposium was to be held.

I was not all nervous except that I do not remember reading my paper or the barrage of questions afterwards. But it seemed that everybody wanted to know about baby hedgehogs and, as all I could give them was personal experience, my paper was, I am told by Russell, very well accepted. As a result of telling people about our hands-on experience I have now been asked to give similar papers to other professional animal groups and at the Royal Veterinary College. This pleases me particularly because, as I am encouraging people to take up wildlife rehabilitation, it's encouraging to know that veterinarians from all over the country, following Russell's example, are willing to give their support to the care of wild animals and birds.

To Be Continued . . .

No one ever gets quite used to standing up in front of an audience and giving talks or, as is happening more frequently for me, presenting papers on specific wildlife rehabilitation topics. Mostly the butterflies recede and the hand steadies after a few minutes but the talk Sue and I are about to give has had us worried for weeks before the event. Not because we are particularly concerned about the exposure, as by now we know our subject inside out. No, the problem is that to get to our venue we have to go by aeroplane. Sue has never flown before but I am sure my blasé attitude will give her every confidence in British Airways – we will fly with no one else. This time it's only a short hop to Guernsey, a mere trifle for a hardened air traveller like me. (Mind you, BA have come up with a way of prolonging the torture by making us pick up a connecting flight in Jersey.)

While we are away, incidentally for the first time since the Hospital was started ten years ago, Colin will stand in for us at home. Russell, of course, will make himself extra-available for emergencies and it will fall on good old Andy to face the wrath of irate swans, foxes, badgers and deer on the heavy rescue front. Most of our long-term intensive care patients will be into convalescence by then. In particular I am thinking of the biters: Sam Fox, Nutkin the little blind squirrel and yet another badger, this time almost cut in half by one of the snares the Minister of the Environment says are not cruel. All these need resolves of steel to handle and I would not enjoy my flights if I thought that they still needed intimate attention.

*A patient
at the hospital.*

Sam Fox is now almost a good-looking fox who growls and snarls as you approach but eight weeks ago was incapable of any resistance. I had to go out and catch him as, because of his severely debilitated state, he had curled up to die in the garage of a semi-detached in High Wycombe. There was an old mattress stored in there in which Sam Fox had chewed a great hole trying to make a comfortable bed to ease his torment. When I first ducked under the up-and-over door I was shocked at his condition and his feeble attempts to hide away from me under an old sideboard. I could feel his agony as I slipped the grasper around his neck and gently lowered him into a carrying basket, pulling away lumps of tortured skin as I lifted his rump. I did not want to cause him any more discomfort but it had to be done – I had to try and help him somehow. In the basket I could take a closer look at him: his eyes, usually so bright and bold in a fox, were dull and almost closed, with dried crusts around his eyelids; his back and tail were devoid of the bright red fur and were a mass of deeply cratered encrustation and dead skin, a severe case of advanced sarcoptic mange caused by the minute mite Sarcoptes. This was only the second case I had ever handled but I was becoming aware of almost an epidemic occurring recently in widespread fox populations.

The recommended procedure with manged foxes, as with so many difficult-to-treat wildlife casualties, had always been the gun or the big needle, but I knew that mange could be cured when it affected dogs and that we had successfully treated many hedgehogs with a similar condition. I made up my mind to cure this fox, as much for his sake as for the others out there and still waiting to be caught. I knew that only then could I go out and shout to the world of 'doubting Thomases': 'You don't need to slaughter manged foxes. They can and should be treated. Give them a chance.'

In its advanced stages, sarcoptic mange must be terribly irritating, which is why infected animals usually die of exhaustion, because they are unable to rest, coupled with starvation because they are too exhausted to hunt or forage. Many people advocate euthanasia because of this irritation, but, as I always point out, with any seriously injured casualty it need only put up with a few more weeks' discomfort before it is free of pain and completely back to normal and

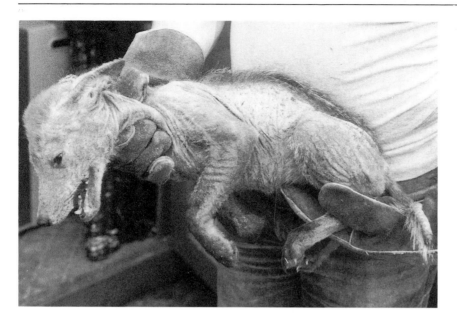

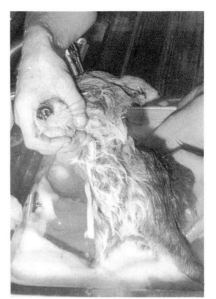

ready to resume a perfectly normal life, probably forgetting its traumatic experiences at the hands of man.

Russell's recommendation for treatment was for Sam Fox to be subjected to a weekly bath of Alugan Concentrate for a minimum of eight weeks. Andy always comes into the Hospital on a Saturday afternoon so it was to be his job to hold Sam Fox, suitably muzzled with a bandage, in the bath while I made sure the Alugan penetrated every square inch of that tortured skin. Sam Fox was so thin and emaciated that as soon as we first wet him all over he seemed to shrink away to nothing, all head with virtually no body, just skin and bone. He looked awful with those great sad eyes pleading pitifully from their sunken sockets but we had to persevere for we knew that even after the first bath he would start to feel better. To make matters worse you must not towel off Alugan; we just had to lay this frightened, shivering fox in a box under a heater and let him drip-dry. He lay there curled up, moaning in deepest misery. I talk about resolve in facing a fit animal but our resolve was facing its fiercest test as the little fox slept, so tiny and bare, in its corner of that enormous box. However, it was not all doom and despondency that day. The Alugan was taking effect and large chunks of that awful crust over his back had disappeared, probably having dissolved away in the bath.

All the following week he just lay in his corner and moaned, oblivious to our changing his bowl of Lectade or cleaning his box. It was soon Saturday afternoon and time for another bath and a close look at his back which was now bare, rather than looking like an old pie crust. Once more, he hung limp in Andy's hands as I bathed him. Afterwards he sank into his corner under the heat lamp but this time he was making feeble attempts to groom himself, licking his legs ever so slowly and deliberately. He was still moaning, almost imperceptibly, but by Tuesday he seemed to stop feeling sorry for himself and was taking note of his surroundings. He still looked like a scarecrow but at least his eyes, although deep in their sockets, were clear of those awful crusts and for the first time he upended his waterbowl and hid it amongst his bedding.

At his third bath he was beginning to look more like a fox and put

Sam Fox before treatment for mange.

When we wet him he seemed to shrink away to nothing.

Sam Fox after treatment.

up quite a struggle, managing to pull the plug out of the sink and letting out all the Alugan. He was still quite shocked for a day or two after the bath but the rest of the week he was pacing his cage ravenously eyeing Mr and Mrs Orange Sauce, the two tufted ducks who lived outside in the fibre-glass pool.

Each Saturday he got more and more difficult for Andy to hold. He has only one more bath to put up with and now has a nice growth of fuzzy baby fur all over his back, although his brush still sticks out behind like a bare branch. He is still in an inside cage and regularly demonstrates his return to fitness and acuity by capitalising on any of my lapses by reaching out and retrieving anything within a foreleg's length of him. To date he has managed to dispose of ceramic heating lamps, twelve foot of three-core cable and the plugs, numerous towels and blankets, the locking-rod from a carrying basket and I am sure many things we have not yet missed.

He is looking good and before he is eventually released I will make sure we have plenty of photographs of his recovery to back me as I know I can now shout with confidence: 'Do not dismiss mangey foxes. They can be cured.'

This is the message we are learning with wildlife casualties. Where in previous years many have been given up as lost we are now able to institute remedies that save lives. Poisoning, however, is still of great concern to us, there being very little chance of identifying a toxin before it is too late. But one major poisoning crisis has been averted by our using fairly basic methods to save the victims and by those champions of a good cause, the media, bringing the public's notice to a potentially disastrous problem.

The crisis first started when Sue Driver, who lived in Luton, made a seventy-mile round trip to bring us two gulls which she had picked up dying on Stewartby Lake near Bedford. Those two however were the tip of the iceberg, we discovered, as Sue described how the lake shore and yacht club lawns and boatyard were littered with dead or dying gulls. Apparently, it was not a new problem and had recurred for some years but the authorities had shown little concern, describing the incidents as a proliferation of botulism caused by the hot weather and the drop in water level.

The weekly menu
at The Wildlife Hospital Summer 1988

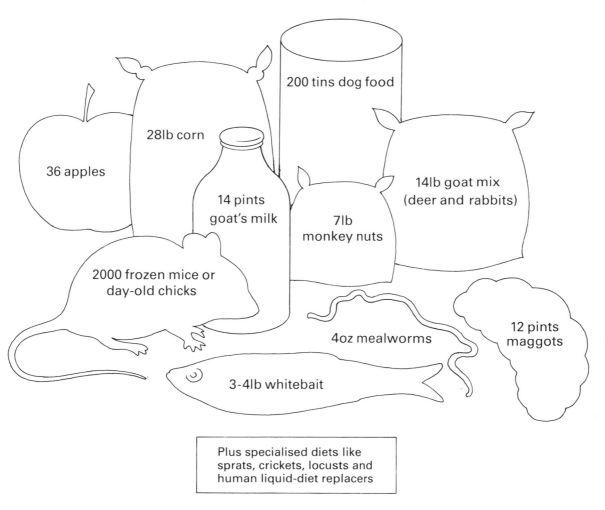

200 tins dog food

28lb corn

36 apples

14lb goat mix
(deer and rabbits)

14 pints
goat's milk

7lb
monkey nuts

2000 frozen mice or
day-old chicks

4oz mealworms

12 pints
maggots

3-4lb whitebait

Plus specialised diets like
sprats, crickets, locusts and
human liquid-diet replacers

Sometimes authority can be callous and in this case nobody bothered about the gasping gulls dying all around them. That is, until Sue came upon the carnage and brought those first two birds over to us.

I had met botulism before and had been successful in treating its toxins by stomach-tubing with a broad-spectrum anti-toxin concocted from John Cooper's book, *First Aid and Care of Wild Birds*. The great theory of this anti-toxin is that one must hit some of the poison and drain it from the body, and follow this by general nursing whereby the body's natural function may, one hopes, leach any residues from the tissues. With the gulls we followed the initial treatment by regular twice-daily tube feeding on a mixture of Complan and Lectade. And it worked.

At least we kept the gulls alive with our first treatments, although neither of them had the strength to stand or even consider feeding themselves. In the meantime, Sue Driver continued to make her daily seventy-mile treks to Stewartby but always she was too late and any new victims were already grotesque corpses being lapped by the waters of the lake. On her third trip she was in time and duly sped to Aylesbury with four more very bedraggled gulls: one lesser blackback and three black-headed. After their initial indignity of being stomach-tubed they were put with the other two, a circle of gulls around a solitary water bowl revelling in the warmth of an overhead heater. None of them could stand up so every few hours we had to run the gauntlet of their sharp bills just to change their flooring.

The following day three more birds, two immature herring gulls and another black-headed, joined our little circle. This was getting ridiculous but the following day there were no new casualties. Perhaps the crisis was over. But the day after, Sue arrived again with two enormous battered cardboard boxes chock full of four enormous lesser black-backs, one herring gull and the inevitable black-headed. This time, though, the larger gulls were all gasping, silently hanging onto life. Could this, I wondered, be a sign of the killer fungus, aspergillus, which accounts for so many sea birds venturing inland? Cramming this latest batch into the incubator to warm, I dosed them all with miconazole, in a vain attempt to counter any aspergillosis. It

The latest batch of gulls in the incubator.

was difficult enough to cope with the botulism, but aspergillus as well meant they did not stand a chance and one by one, in a matter of an hour or so, the five large gulls had breathed their last.

Sue Driver was now exhausted from her efforts so Trevor and I donned our wellies and went to see for ourselves. Stewartby Lake is an enormous expanse of water created from old brick workings, millions of which form the shore and made it very difficult for us to inspect every nook and cranny. On the water, in the distance were literally hundreds of gulls, while not far from the shore sailed flotillas of very healthy swans, including a black vagrant – not from Australia, surely? All sorts of ducks, coots and moorhens dabbled and dived in the shallows but these all looked very healthy. Yet all around the shore were corpses of seagulls. Why?

Knowing the habits of gulls I began to come up with my theory that there was nothing wrong with Stewartby itself. The gulls were obviously flying off to feed elsewhere, only returning there to roost and, in many cases, to die. The authorities once again had a simple answer: the gulls were feeding on a nearby household tip, picking up the poison, if it was botulism, from decaying food and other organic waste. I did not believe this for a minute. Gulls, to my knowledge, are like crows and have cast-iron constitutions, being able to eat practically anything without suffering ill effects. That was not the answer: there was something we were not being told. As it was, Trevor and I found no sick gulls that day, only the dead.

The following morning the possible answer glared at me, over the breakfast table, from the pages of *The Mail on Sunday*. 'Swiss use Britain as chemical dump' screamed the headline above an article about toxic materials being imported and dumped at an open site at, you've guessed it, Stewartby. This was not the natural botulism toxin we had been led to believe was the cause of the gulls' death; this was waste including 'lead, cadmium, mercury and dioxin, the deadly poison involved in the Seveso disaster in Italy in 1976'. *The Mail* campaigned and the deadly import traffic was halted but that open death-trap, the pit, was still there. We thought it was all over but another black-headed gull was recently picked up near Stewartby, displaying the same symptoms of goodness-knows what poison. I am hearing again reports of dead or dying gulls. Are the people who use Stewartby blind to what's going on? A disgraceful sign is apparently festooned on the yacht club wall: 'Don't handle the sick birds'. Why not? Might they carry the poison man has dumped for them? I say to everybody who passes Stewartby Lake, stop and have a look for sick gulls. Pick them up in an old newspaper if you are worried. But pick them up you must and, if you can, get them to us as soon as possible.

We managed to save and release, on safer waters, about fifty per cent of those gulls and the latest herring gull, which I rescued myself, is responding well to treatment. Whenever I am in the Bedford area now, I make a detour for a quick walk around Stewartby. This most recent poison victim was found because I had rendezvoused with Wincey Willis at junction 13 on the M1 to pick up an injured kestrel which Russell was to work on, and junction 13 is only a few miles

About 50% of those gulls were saved and released.

Rescue Centre

Necessary off-site rescue boats, vehicles and equipment will be held at-the-ready, together with workshops in which to build and maintain the various pens and housing for recuperating patients.

All boundaries will be planted with hedges of native British species.

A horticultural centre will be established to maintain the grounds and pens and to establish trial grounds for propagating declining species.

Staff Accommodation

Offering permanent and substitute manning of the Hospital at all times, day and night.

Administration Area

Comprising the necessary office, casualty reception and a student registration centre, with a sales area to promote the Trust's own merchandise.

The Veterinary Unit

Incorporating prep room, theatre, X-ray and isolation. The latest veterinary and laboratory techniques can be implemented in order to treat the whole vista of British wildlife.

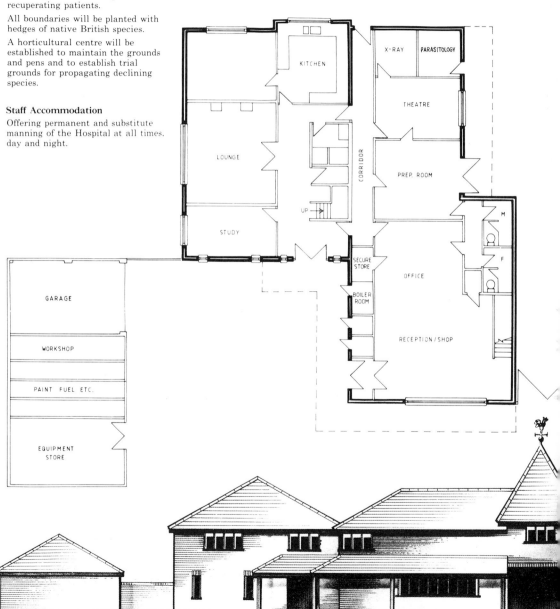

Food Preparation and Storage

Incorporating foodstore, prep kitchen and insect breeder, with freezer and refrigeration storage facilities coupled with the facility to breed certain insect foods vital to many birds and small mammals.

Parasitology Unit

To establish and record previously unknown diseases carried by wildlife.

A nature trail will be laid to allow school parties to view some of the residents without disturbing them.

Area for outside heated and filtered rehabilitation pool for water birds and mammals.

Standing for pens, including those for the breeding and release of butterflies, insects, birds and small mammals.

Intensive Care

Individually designed to cope with the many facets of the different species arriving at the Hospital.

Oiled and Large Bird Operations Unit

Comprising a washroom, recovery, pool room designed on tried and tested lines to cope with oil-spill disasters and the many other water bird problems, particularly swans and herons, encountered throughout the year.

Oiled-Bird and Badger Reception Unit

Comprised of many easily-maintained individual compartments that can house quantities of oiled sea birds or larger mammals, such as badgers, foxes and deer.

Education Centre (First floor)

Illustrated lectures backed with a full and comprehensive reference library of literature and visual aids will be available to students at all levels.

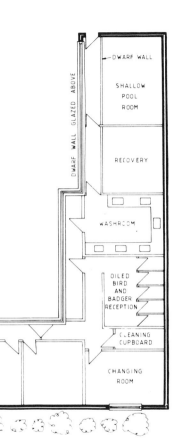

Ground floor
(First floor not shown)

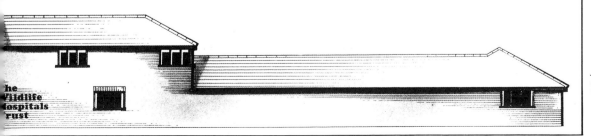

*Plan for the Wildlife
Teaching Hospital.*

from the infamous lake. I was there for only about half an hour in a blinding rainstorm but I still managed to find the gull clinging to the edge of land by his bill, as the water threatened to drag him under. I was quite unprepared for my little excursion and stuffed him up my jumper as I made my way back to the car. All the way home he sat under the heater and it saved his life.

Please try to walk round Stewartby if you are round that way. We will always take any casualty and try to save it.

Wincey is one of the stalwarts of our newly launched Appeal to build Europe's first wildlife teaching hospital. In Britain alone I estimate that there are millions of wildlife casualties every year and it's horrifying to realise that ninety-five per cent of these happen as a result of encounters with man and his effects on the countryside. Cats alone are responsible for one hundred million. Even at full stretch we, at Aylesbury, could never cope with such horrendous numbers but wouldn't it be wonderful if other people were to open up their own wildlife hospitals all over the country? Only then would we be able even to attempt to tackle the problem.

However, it's not that easy and at times you seem to be taking one step forward and two back; but the release of just one, fit again casualty makes all the heartache worthwhile. At the new hospital complex we shall have facilities to invite veterinarians, their nurses and students, potential and established wildlife rescuers onto courses where we can impart the knowledge and experience we have gained over the years not just in animal welfare topics but also in the crucial field of administration and finance which has been the downfall of so many other rescue centres. Add to this the rich interchange of information between students and we can begin to make an impression on those millions of casualties. We started and coped for many years in a tiny back garden, so you do not need acres and acres of land to take in wildlife casualties. In fact, the little old lady on the corner who just looks after ten blackbirds a year is as important a cog in the wheel as the large rescue centre which handles hundreds.

We all must act now to reduce the casualty figures. No wildlife population, however large, can stand these horrendous losses and many slow-breeding species are already in trouble, being unable to

reproduce fast enough to cope with the problem. How long will it be before that enigma that we are all a part of, the so-called natural balance, starts to disintegrate?

However, people do respond to warnings and cries for help. Following our work on hedgehogs I have seen people all over the country caring for the prickly characters. The British people are best with their backs to the wall and judging by the hedgehog experience I know that the new wildlife teaching hospital will be as successful in its teaching as it will be in looking after casualties.

Ten years ago when Sue and I started taking in wildlife casualties our crusade for the sick and injured was largely ignored by conservation bodies. Yet so great has been the public's response to our work that many of the groups have been forced to change their opinions. The injured wild bird now has a list of telephone numbers which you can call for help; hedgehog wards are springing up all over the country and even UNESCO, one of the largest charities in the world, called on me in my little corner of Buckinghamshire to read publicly one of the 'Stories For A Prince' to be presented to Prince Harry. Mind you, I was probably called on because the story told of an animal in a predicament that would have taxed even my powers of initiative and improvisation: a hippopotamus with a fruit bowl stuck on its bottom.

On thinking about it, I do get so many seemingly ludicrous calls about animals in ridiculous situations that I could probably have found a solution. Birds fallen down behind gas fires, hedgehogs down drains, badgers in all manner of silly positions, such as up behind the dashboard of a car or ravelled up in a goal net, and, most recently, a 'townie' pigeon which had succeeded in halting the everturning wheels of British justice, are all part of a typical day's phone calls to Aylesbury.

The pigeon in question had somehow taken up residence in the lofty ceiling of Aylesbury's brand new Crown Court. The visiting judge had adjourned all proceedings until the incursor had been apprehended or shot. The Clerk of the Court preferred the former, less drastic course of action and phoned us for advice. I suggested that he put some food in the ante-chamber, but visible from the main courtroom, to lure the pigeon out. I assumed he would put down some type of birdseed but the Clerk, having had no experience of birds, promptly went to the nearby sandwich bar and purchased one round of 'cheese in white'. This he laid temptingly on the floor of the ante-chamber.

But this pigeon was a wise old bird who was not going to fall for the 'bait on the floor' ploy and merely continued preening on his lofty perch on the frieze around the ceiling. Consequently I was then summoned out to help.

I have a swan net which, when fully extended, is eleven foot long. The only trouble is that it then becomes completely uncontrollable. In any case, even with it extended and me flailing about with my arms outstretched I still could not reach the frieze.

The Clerk, in his sober court clothes, then added his own refined improvisation by throwing feather dusters in an attempt to disturb the bird. It flew once to the public gallery but even as I thought about catching it there, it returned to its Masada, its impregnable fortress in the ceiling. However, I had worked out a way of reaching it, though it meant balancing a stool between the Judge's chair and a wall seat, an action I hoped would not be interpreted as contempt. Balancing on one leg over the bench and with my net outstretched above me, threatening to bring my construction tumbling down, I managed at last to dislodge the pigeon. It promptly took refuge above the far more accessible public gallery where I was able to stalk it, net it and finally release it into the Market Square to join all the other pigeons. He might even have been a descendant of those town pigeons which I had saved ten years before.

It's just as well that this pigeon was not injured in my clambering because to have had to bring it back to the Hospital would have put even more stress on our bulging seams and growing family of pigeons.

As you walk around the Hospital you are likely to trip over six pigeons which cannot fly, for one reason or another. They are no trouble but one sometimes threatens our domestic stability when it tries to set up house in the kitchen. Somehow I know, instinctively, every sound that emanates from my patients. Whether it's Purdie,

The lapwing 'pee-witting' for no reason.

who is now eleven years old, demanding more food for her five babies or whether it's the lapwing 'pee-witting' for no reason or the incessant squeaking of the three almost fully grown coots, I know every 'peep'. At least until one day last week, when I walked past the outside fence and heard a strange squeaking coming from the corner by the deer pen. I thought that it might be a mouse which had moved into the hay with our latest muntjac casualty or a family of blue tits nesting in the fence but I could find nothing. It's always the same: if you hear a noise and go to investigate it, the noise stops. In intensive care it's not unusual to hear a hedgehog cough but when you approach the banks of hospital cages, silence reigns supreme. It was the same with this squeaking until one unguarded little 'peep' had me on my knees peering under the rabbit hutches. There, in the darkest corner between the hutches and the deer pen, was a charming avian family picture of two of our resident grounded pigeons with two cute ugly babies which had escaped detection for at least five days. They had been very lucky as we daily hose the whole ground area and it's a wonder they had not been flushed away. Now we have a large sign above the hutches, 'Ne Hosez Pas', which should save them from a dousing until they are ready to fly away.

I spend most of my time in the garden with the Hospital and its patients. Most of our casualties arrive during the evening and, as I wait, in my small First Aid unit, for the latest hedgehog casualty to unroll, I can sense the 'night shift' taking over. We have had a run this year on those cuties, young tawny owls, and they are now wide awake hissing at each other and the two hedgehogs, Anneka and Patches II, which share their pen. Before you all panic, adult hedgehogs are never molested by tawny owls. In the next pen Purdie and her chicks are snuggled down for the night, while around the corner I can hear Biddy and Granny chomping on their meals and opposite them there's the scratching from the pens of the three young foxes recovering from orthopaedic operations. Chestnut, the squirrel, comes out for a midnight drink and my hedgehog unrolls as the doorbell buzzes to herald the arrival of the next casualty.

Postscript
1988–9

Most wild creatures are tough and resilient but sometimes, when hurt, just need a helping hand to get them back on the right tracks.

We are building Europe's first wildlife teaching hospital, **The Wild Care Centre**, which is going to cost £1,100,000 to include facilities to cope with any wildlife emergency as well as, possibly, some chance of salvation for the stricken seals in the North Sea.

So far we have received tremendous support from the British Petroleum Company. plc, British Telecom, Hedgehog Foods, The Body Shop and many other companies. We have raised a quarter of our appeal target and will soon be laying the first brick.

So, if you can see your way to helping us achieve the new wildlife teaching hospital, please get in touch, and, it goes without saying, that if you need help with a casualty, contact us at:

> The Wildlife Hospital Trust
> (incorporating St Tiggywinkles)
> Enquiries C B
> 1 Pemberton Close
> Aylesbury
> Bucks HP21 7NY

To be continued . . .

OPERATION OTTER
Philip Wayre

Otters are wild, fascinating, and endangered. But thanks to Philip Wayre and his wife Jeanne they are at last returning to England's waterways. From his first sighting of an otter in a Norfolk dawn, this wonderful story follows Philip Wayre's dream – from his early filming of otters to the setting up of an otter reserve and, finally, the culmination – the successful and safe release of groups of young otter cubs into the wild.

Operation Otter is moving, appealing and practical, full of irresistible photos and a wealth of information about the otter itself.

The Secret Life of The
NEW FOREST
Eric Ashby
Introduction by Richard Mabey

In this enchanting book of colour photographs, the secrets of one of Britain's oldest and most beautiful forests are revealed. The wild and natural aspects of the Forest through the changing seasons – from giant oaks to deer and ponies, from fox cubs, badgers and pigs to woodpeckers, rare orchids and butterflies – are observed with infinite patience, love and more than a touch of genius by a man who has photographed wildlife for over fifty years and lives deep in the New Forest.

THE FLOWERING OF BRITAIN
Richard Mabey & Tony Evans

The Flowering of Britain is a magnificent celebration of the wild flowers of Britain and the part they have played in our culture for eight thousand years.

Richard Mabey's fresh look at our best-known flowers, at their distribution, history and legends, has been stunningly illustrated with photographs by Tony Evans.

THE COMPLETE HEDGEHOG
Les Stocker
Foreword by John Craven

Everyone loves hedgehogs. Here is the most comprehensive book ever written about this endearing mammal, one of nature's greatest assets.

Les Stocker presents, in this fully illustrated, magical book, information about the hedgehog's history, mythology, distribution, habits and habitat, as well as practical advice on how to unroll a hedgehog, how to encourage one to your garden, what to do about orphan hedgehogs and how to treat casualties.